Praise for *Step into Syn...*

"Carol's book empowers every person to create a new way of being, a new vibration, a new way of life and a new future. I have now lived in this new world as laid out by Carol in 'Step into Synchronicity' for several years, and believe me, everything she says is true. YOU have the power within to change your entire world. Read her book, trust the process"

— Michael Dennis

"Carol guides the reader through a beautifully descriptive text about how to allow the divine essence into one's life. Her book has something to teach someone at any level of practice, providing readers with practical advice about how to overcome obstacles in their path in order to fully realize their true power and manifesting potential."

- Kelsey Bennett, LMSW

"Carol's experiences will make you a believer and her guidance will have you co-creating infinite possibilities and probabilities in your life. You will be amazed at what you will begin to manifest when you follow Carol's wisdom provided in this book. Remember, the Divine has your back!"

— Stacey Haluka, Author of
The Unspoken Truth About Essential Oils

"I have learned so much working with Carol. She helped me find courage to transition out of a job that was stale in my life. I've learned to tap into Divine guidance with her help. And I've drafted off of her faith as I was taking steps to grow in my own life. The steps outlined in this book will increase your awareness, increase your connection to Divine and show you how to move forward in your life."

- Nancy Sutherland

STEP INTO SYNCHRONICITY

Dancing with the Divine to Create Magic
and Miracles in Your Life

By Carol Cowan

Disclaimer:
By reading this book you assume full responsibility for how
you choose to use this content. The information contained in
this book is provided for educational purposes only and is not
intended to replace qualified medical supervision.

For further information, please contact:
Email: info@carolcowan.ca
Web: www.carolcowan.ca

For Olivia, my most precious gift.

Carol Cowan

TABLE OF CONTENTS:

INTRODUCTION

Ladies and gentlemen...this is your dance teacher speaking. It's time to put your dance shoes on and prepare for a very valuable dance lesson. You're about to take a magical and enlightening lesson on what I like to call the "dance floor of life". Please make a conscious choice about partaking in this lesson as it requires a certain level of commitment and open-mindedness. Once you're on the dance floor, there's no getting off either. I repeat, this dance lesson is infinite and only picks up new dancers along the way. No one ever leaves the dance floor as the lessons are ever unfolding. I guarantee that there will be some challenges along the way and lots of unexpected twists and turns as some of the dance moves are complicated and require deeper levels of awareness. Therefore, properly fitted dance shoes are required.

While you're on this dance floor, you'll be asked to take some lessons in Dancing with the Divine Universe. You will learn how to let go of control, to be in the present moment and let the Divine guide you to lead the life you were meant to live. Dancing with the Divine is a beautiful experience once you learn the proper steps and can relax into the process. To "dance" means to move rhythmically.... usually to music, but in this case, it will feel more like living a life in rhythm with the pulse of the Universe. To connect with that "something" that is greater than us, to get out of our own way, and let that "something greater" guide us, lead us and provide us with miracles, one dance step at a time. Other lessons you will be taking while on this dance floor include meditation, yoga, Emotional Freedom Technique and how to consciously create your reality. Hope you brought your notebook and yoga mat!

In case of emergency, you will notice that your dance teacher is there on the floor with you, ready to guide you every step of the way and support you if you fall. The process of learning to dance takes time and patience, and your teacher is willing to help you along the way. In addition to the teacher, for the entire time on this floor, there is also a wonderful companion, confidant, and friend. This companion loves you intensely and unconditionally. This companion already knows everything about you and is always all around you. At no point does this companion ever leave your side while on this dance floor. In fact, the longer you stay on this dance floor, the more you will be able to feel and experience the loving presence of this Divine Companion. After some practice, you and this Divine companion, (aka The Universe), will be flowing and dancing together with effortless grace and ease. It is this companion that you'll be taking the dance lessons with.

You will also come across other people on this dance floor that are currently learning to dance with the Divine Universe, dealing with whatever comes up as they stumble trying to learn new moves. Just like you, these other dancers are typically filled with limiting beliefs, painful memories, and a history. Please treat them with kindness and compassion as you don't know their story. Everyone experiences the moves and turns on this dance floor differently. The longer you're on the floor, and the better you get at dancing with the Divine, the smaller the stumbles will seem and the easier the turns will feel. You will learn to go with the flow and the turns along the way will likely result in joyous laughter. In the meantime, feel free to mindfully assist other people on the dance floor in whatever way you see fit and appropriate, if that person is open to receiving help and that you offer help with genuine kindness.

Be aware that many coincidences and synchronicities tend to occur for people while on this dance floor. These are moments where you will be left in a state of awe and wonderment as the event that just occurred was so unlikely that you know the Divine Universe must have had a hand in arranging it. You are encouraged to truly appreciate these moments so that they may occur more and more often while on the dance floor. You will also learn the steps required to cultivate such experiences in your life on a more frequent basis.

This is a final warning that learning to dance with the Divine Universe, while on this infinite dance floor of awareness, will inevitably produce feelings of total trust, immense love, and boundless bliss. Your life is guaranteed to change forever in ways that you cannot possibly imagine in this present moment. You've just got to get on the floor, let go of any expectations, and enjoy the dance. So, if you're ready, tighten up those dance shoes because the dance lessons of infinite awareness will begin now....

CHAPTER 1:

THE ONLY WAY OUT OF DARKNESS IS TO DANCE TOWARDS THE LIGHT

It is my deepest desire that you live a life full of peace, joy, and happiness. It is my wish that you come to understand it is possible to live a life free from suffering. When we are connected to the Divine Universe, we have the opportunity to be free of fear, anxiety and the desire to control every outcome in our lives. We have an opportunity to simply trust the process of life and flow with ease. Each one of us on this planet has this opportunity, while we are here in physical form, to move from darkness to light, from unawareness to pure awareness. Our mission, should we choose to accept it, is to connect with the deepest desire in our hearts, open and trust the Divine Universe as we learn to consciously co-create our life with the Divine. This book, should you choose to read it in its entirety and practice the methods within it, will guide you from a life of suffering to a life full of magic and miracles.

Living in darkness is also known as being unconscious, unaware, or living and operating from past conditioning and we've all been there! So, how do you know when you're in the darkness? You may be in the darkness and not even be aware that you are. Or perhaps you've just come to realize that you've been living in the darkness, unaware and unconscious, and you're just starting to wake up now. Just like how most of us naturally wake up when the sunlight starts shining in our bedroom in the morning and we start by stretching and rubbing our eyes, the process of becoming more conscious and more aware takes time.

Or perhaps, you're at the part where you're wondering why life is so challenging and difficult most of the time? You've tried everything outside of yourself to bring yourself happiness, but it seems that no amount of material things such as gambling, alcohol, time on the internet, food or shopping really seem to bring you deep and lasting happiness. And so, you've started to ask some bigger questions.

At the same time, there may be some of you who have already started to raise your level of awareness, move towards the light, and established a connection with the Divine. And if so, keep going because the journey from darkness to light is truly infinite.

Regardless of where you are, a whole other level of peace, light, and love graciously awaits you every waking moment. This light, also known as the Divine, is the only way out of the darkness. The Divine is always patiently waiting to connect with you. It loves you unconditionally and more than you could possibly comprehend. It wants, more than anything, for you to be happy and to co-create a gracious, beautiful life together. However, since we have free will, we get to choose. We get to choose if we want to suffer, do it all on our own, and struggle. God knows I did that for years! (More details on that in a later chapter…stay tuned). All the while, as we are struggling and fumbling in the darkness, doing everything on our own, dancing by ourselves, tripping over our own feet, the Divine lovingly watches and patiently waits by our side. If we do not pray, meditate, ask for help or open ourselves up to receive, the Divine can only assume that we are choosing to execute our free will and therefore allows us to steer our own course. If we choose to ask, we shall receive.

So, at this point, you might be thinking, "What?! You mean this whole time there has been an incredible, all-knowing, powerful force within me and all around me that has the ability if I choose to connect with it, to assist me in living a life filled with grace, ease, trust, and peace? Why didn't you tell me?" If I would have told you sooner, you would not have been ready or open to learning how to dance with the Divine. However, the very fact that you're holding this book in your hand indicates that you're ready now.

I should warn you that this process of transitioning from darkness to light is not always easy. You know that moment when you first open your eyes in the morning and the sun is shining so brightly that it almost hurts your eyes? And so, you close them tightly again and roll over trying to go back to sleep? That's what it's going to feel like sometimes. That's what some people do. And that's okay because it's not always easy or pleasant. There have been many times that I just want to roll over and go back to sleep too! But I should also tell you that this trip from darkness to light, from unconscious to conscious, from being alone to being deeply connected to the Divine, is a bit of a paradox. It will likely be the most challenging process you'll experience while living in this plane of the Universe, but it will also, without a doubt, be the most magical and worthwhile experience you'll ever have. Once you move towards the light and learn to dance graciously, life becomes easy, blissful and full of wonder every day. You will know and feel in every waking moment that you are loved unconditionally and that there is nothing to worry about...ever. And that, in my personal experience, is priceless.

The process of moving from darkness to light is similar to learning anything new. Learning to be in harmony with the Divine is a skill that can be cultivated by anyone willing to learn. It will require dedication and take practice so that you can be connected and in flow more often. Being "in flow" with the Divine, when it happens for you, will feel like a partner leading you on a dance floor. Learning any skill takes time, whether that is learning to dance Salsa, play the piano, draw, cook or connect to the Divine Universe. There will be stages or phases that you will go through. This process of learning to connect with the Divine is best described using The Four Stages of Competence Model by Abraham Maslow.

There are four basic stages of learning any new skill: Unconscious Incompetence, Conscious Incompetence, Conscious Competence, and Unconscious Competence. In order to learn or change in any way, we must first become conscious of our incompetence in whatever areas we desire growth. When we first become aware of what we're not good at—for example, managing our finances if we're in debt, or playing an instrument if we never have—it tends to bring up feelings of weakness and inadequacy. And we don't like those feelings. An awareness of what skills we lack is a very normal part of any process of learning and development. Let's take a closer look at each of the four stages of learning as it applies to the process of developing a connection to the Divine. When you know what's ahead of you, you can avoid feeling discouraged because you will know that it's just part of the process.

1. **Unconscious incompetence (A.K.A. Totally in the Dark)**

In this stage, we don't know what we don't know. Let's first imagine learning a skill like salsa dancing (or playing the piano or any other skill). Initially, the individual is often unaware that they do not understand or know how to do something because no situations have ever come up to make the individual aware of this deficit. He or she often knows there is a skill lacking but denies the usefulness of the skill. The individual must recognize their own incompetence and the possible value of the new skill, before moving on to the next stage. The length of time an individual spends in this stage depends on how necessary it is for one to learn. The individual must experience an increase in motivation to add new skills to their list. For example, you have yet to come across a reason in your life that would require you to know how to dance salsa or play the piano, so you never consider it.

Now let's imagine that we're struggling in life or experiencing a deeper sense of emptiness inside that nothing seems to fill. Our life is often filled with a roller coaster of emotions including fear, anxiety, and fleeting moments of happiness. In this stage, we typically feel frustrated, overwhelmed or a sense of lack. We likely have no connection with the Divine or even a desire to connect with the Divine as we may be unaware of that potential - we are unaware, that we are unaware. If someone were to introduce us to the concept of connecting with the Divine as a path of healing, we may reject that as an option.

2. Conscious incompetence (A.K.A. The break of Dawn)

This is the stage where the individual typically becomes aware that they do not understand or know how to do something. They also begin to recognize this lack is important and it would be valuable to learn new skills in order to deal with the shortfall and gain competence. The making of mistakes may be frequent and is central to the learning process at this stage as the individual refines the skills through practice. For example, you are invited to attend a wedding in Cuba where everyone knows how to dance salsa, and they all dance very well...except for you. At the reception you find yourself becoming acutely aware of your two left feet and inability to dance. Your friend pulls you onto the dance floor and starts to show you the basics and you try to follow but do more fumbling than anything else.

Similarly, this is the part where we start to wake up. We meet others who used to feel the same way about life, often struggling or feeling frustrated, disconnected and empty. Somehow, they started to connect with the Divine and they now experience more magic and miracles in their life. As they explain how wonderful their life is now you start to contemplate if a life like that would be possible for you. You listen to their recommendations about meditation and prayer and start to become more open and self-reflective as well. You start to realize that maybe connecting with the Divine is the way to living a more peaceful life but still feel a bit confused about how that might all happen for you. As you begin to start a silent meditation practice you experience some frustration but are curious to learn more.

3. **Conscious competence (A.K.A. The Light Shining Through)**

In this stage, the individual understands or knows how to engage in the skill. They can demonstrate the skill or knowledge, but it requires focus, concentration, and effort. It may need to be broken down into steps or detailed processes. There is often heavy conscious involvement involved executing the new skill. The frequency of mistakes begins to decline. For example, you've committed yourself to learn how to dance salsa so that the next time you head to a wedding or an all-inclusive resort in the Caribbean you can light up the dance floor! You decided to take dance lessons three times a week and, six months later, you're finally feeling the rhythm. A great deal of focus is required whenever you're on the floor. Your dance teacher will support you and encourage you every time you make a mistake.

Likewise, in the process of connecting with the Divine, you're starting to experience moments of silence and brief states of bliss during your meditation practice. You start to notice coincidences and synchronicities happening for you, such as when you think of someone and then they call you. You also start to notice small miracles in your life that allow you to feel trust in some Divine essence. These moments of synchronicity and being connected to a Divine essence seem to come and go at random though, which makes you start to wonder if it's possible to live in this state of flow more often and, if so, how?

4. **Unconscious competence (A.K.A. Living fully in the light and connected to the Divine)**

This is the stage where the individual has had so much refining practice with a skill that they do not really need to think about what to do. It has become "second nature" or automatic and can be performed with a very low frequency of errors. Since the skill is not occupying much of the individual's conscious thoughts, it can often be performed while executing another task if necessary. The individual has become so comfortable with the skill that they will often be able to teach it to others as well.

For example, a few years have now gone by now and you've kept up consistently with your salsa dance lessons. You feel like you're on fire when you're on the dance floor and it shows! At the same time, when you're dancing with the right partner, an amazing state occurs where you are totally in flow together. At this point, you now have an ability to simply allow your movement to be an expression of the music you hear, as it moves through your body. Those who are watching can even feel the magic that happens when you're in this state and they applaud at the end of the song....and you take a bow.

In this stage of connecting with the Divine, life becomes a mystical and magical experience every day. More often, if not all day long, you feel your connection to the Divine and dance graciously together. You look forward to your meditation every day as it has become a practice that you now enjoy, and it is how you connect with the Divine. Coincidences and synchronicities of Divine timing don't even surprise you anymore as they have simply become a way of life. Miracles occur on a consistent basis and seem to fulfill your every need at just the right time. And when you're not feeling in flow, you know exactly how to relax and get connected to the Divine again. You have mastered the art of dancing with the Divine and life couldn't be more beautiful.

In this process of learning there likely came a moment when you realized that the simple act of connecting with the Divine also required an act of surrendering on your part. A realization that this all-knowing, all-powerful, ever-present, loving Divine energy, truly longs to connect with you and guide you through the process of life. It truly desires to support your soul in finding and staying on the path that your soul wanted to experience before arriving on this earth. It is a delicate dance.... a very delicate dance. And with trust in your heart, you made a conscious choice to acquiesce to the Divine. And it was the best decision ever.

The more you practice anything, the easier it gets. And the easier it gets, the easier it gets! This means that the more you practice dancing with the Divine and connecting to Spirit the more that it will simply become your way of life. The process will feel like moving out of the darkness and into the light, from resistance to acquiescence, from struggle to serendipity, and from forcing to allowing.

> *"The secret of change is to focus all of*
> *your energy, not on fighting the old, but*
> *on building the new"*
> *~ Socrates*

What does that really mean? As mentioned before, we as human beings tend to be creatures of habit. If you don't currently have a habit of living life in effortless co-creation with the Divine, then you must develop the pattern of doing that (don't worry, this book will show you how to do that). You may currently have a pattern of struggling, forcing, worrying, trying to do everything yourself or another negative pattern that blocks the flow of Divine energy and guidance in your life. Maybe you're reading this book because you've become aware of that and would like to change that. This is not necessarily considered to be an easy process. In fact, significant change can be one of the most challenging things to accomplish so it's important to go easy on yourself during the process. At the same time, the good news is that if you are the one who experiences the pattern of a certain negative emotion, then you can change it. In fact, you are the only one who can change it as the change happens from the inside out, not the other way around. If you created a negative pattern, it means you can create a new more positive pattern. And once you practice that new pattern, repeatedly, that will become your new way of life. This new pattern will then begin to manifest itself in the vibrational energy that surrounds you which is when your life then begins to reflect that back to you. Maybe you've been practicing feeling negative for a long time. Now it's time to start practicing connecting with the Divine!

So instead of resisting your current state of reality and the range of negative emotions you might experience on a regular basis, the first trick is to first come to a state of complete acceptance of where you're at today and then as often as you can, do your best to stop operating from that "old pattern". By old pattern I mean to stop telling the same story repeatedly if it's not serving you. Stop living in the past and return your focus and attention to the present moment as often as you can. Just do your best to avoid strengthening old negative patterns by becoming aware of the thought pattern that triggers them. Begin to guide your thoughts in a different direction before the negative emotions connected to those thoughts start to spiral out of control. Sometimes we think if we focus on trying to fix the problem or the negative emotion, we can make it go away. Or we contemplate, examine or try to figure out when this negative pattern started in our life, never really deciding to see the situation differently or tell the story a different way. This just keeps you in the state of darkness.

In order to start moving towards the light, the second trick is to practice the new pattern or the new way of being, repeatedly. The new way of being that you will be learning in this book is the art of dancing with the Divine. Of course, you are also encouraged to practice happiness, joy, relaxation, peace, contentment, gratitude, appreciation, love or any other emotion that you would like to be predominant in your life.

The simple act of practicing feeling a certain way will allow that pattern or skill to strengthen and eventually become your natural pattern or vibration. This also means that if you make it a habit or pattern of connecting with the Divine, magic, and miracles can be a regular part of your life. Just like that! Being guided, listening and following through with the guidance you receive from the Divine is just a skill like any other. Once you practice and become more proficient at seeing the subtle signs and feeling the gentle nudges that the Divine provides, you're on your way to living a magical life full of grace and ease.

How do I know that you might ask?

I offer this information from a place of deeper understanding and have had real life experience with this process. I know that if it was possible for me to move from a dark place of being unconscious and unaware to a place of truly feeling blessed and connected to the Divine every day then it is possible for you too. There is a place in my heart that truly longs for all other beings to be free, happy and full of peace. Having been raised in a home by a mother who struggled with severe mental health issues and a father who drank alcohol daily, I felt I had no choice but to start dancing with the Divine at the age of 18. I knew that there had to be a more peaceful way to live life. Years later, I would find that what I was really looking for was within me the entire time. This aspect of the Divine was patiently waiting within my heart center and all around me, longing to connect with me. And so, I practiced. Every time I had a small coincidence, serendipity, or miraculous event happen in my life, I wrote it down in my journal and told as many people as I could (even though a small part of me initially wondered if they would think I was a little weird.) The reason I wrote every event down, no matter how small, is because I knew that I was strengthening the pattern of creating more magic and miracles. I loved every moment of living my life in flow and dancing with the Divine that I wanted to experience life like that every day. Knowing that whatever we focus our attention on continues to grow and expand in our lives, I decided to focus on miracles and the Divine timing of coincidences. In six months, I had written over two hundred experiences. Now…I've lost count because it's simply a way of life for me. My heart was filled with joy and love to the point that I only long for others to live their life this way, should they so choose. I'm not saying that it's been an easy path, but I am saying that it's possible. It will require that you learn how to focus your attention, to maintain your attention, and to let go of attachment to a particular outcome at the same time.

To further understand how to strengthen a new pattern I will invite you to use a visual picture. Imagine that you and your dance partner have been dancing the Tango for a few years now. As you and your partner have been practicing the Tango, you have become intertwined energetically, you know how to read every subtle lead that they offer, and you dance very well together. The more that you practice together, the more you can refine your movements and make the dance look effortless. Dancing the Tango is like practicing any skill, habit or way of being. The more you dance the Tango, the more that you strengthen that pattern. However, one day you realize that the

25

Tango is not for you anymore and that you would like to explore a new style of dance. You start to practice dancing the Waltz instead and find a new love for this style of dance. The Waltz looks and feels completely different than the Tango, but with focus and practice, you become better at the Waltz and float easily and elegantly on the dance floor. You strengthen the pattern of movement associated with the Waltz and soon enough you have refined the skill.

The important question to ask is what type of dance have you been doing?

If you've been dancing a dance of negative emotion or living a life disconnected from the Divine for a long time, then all you have to do is stop dancing that way and decide you don't want to Tango anymore. The most important part is to start a new dance; a type of dance that you love and enjoy…a habit or pattern that serves you well, a life of being connected to the Divine and keep your attention on that style of dance as you continue to learn and practice it. Keep your eyes glued to that new type of dance as if it's the most important thing in the world because it is. As you keep dancing the new style of your choice, guess what happens to the Tango dance you walked away from? You forget those moves…just like that.

Practicing the new way of being and living a life more connected to the Divine is ultimately the only thing you need to do. Your old way of being and patterns of negative emotions will do their best to distract your attention and pull you back into the old song and dance, but you have to say to them in your mind…sorry, I choose to dance with the Divine instead!

So how long exactly will this process take?

The answer is that there is no magic timeframe as it really depends on several different factors. It could take months, years, a lifetime or even multiple lifetimes for some people. The point is to essentially enjoy the whole process of it all. You will have some amazing, magical moments along the way or finally overcome some challenge that has been blocking you in life for a long time. But that's not the end of it. I promise. It just means that once the Divine guides you through a profoundly synchronistic day or assists you to overcome an obstacle, keep in mind that more profound days are still to come, and more obstacles will still lay in your future. Fortunately, or unfortunately, there is no actual destination that will ever feel final. There is only infinite evolution. All the challenges and mystical experiences are for the purpose of your soul's infinite growth and to explore your true potential while you're here this time around.

Keeping that in mind, some factors that determine the length of time include your willingness and openness to learn and change. Are you putting the covers back over your head when the light begins to shine in the window in the morning? Or do you stretch your arms, hop out of bed and open the curtains? The choice is up to you. Being human means you're likely a creature of habit and change requires conscious attention and focus. The time it takes may also depend on your level of dedication to the process, including how often you practice silence, prayer or meditation. Finding a spiritual teacher along your path can certainly help with this process. Who you choose to associate with is another determining factor. It is recommended to spend as much time as possible with like-minded people also on their journey from darkness to light so that you can help each other along the way as opposed to people who are negative or still hanging out in the blissfully unaware state of darkness.

Finally, the best way I can possibly describe the unfolding of this process from darkness to light is to imagine you're on the dance floor with someone. To be more specific, let's imagine that you're on the dance floor of a beautiful ballroom dance studio, with stain glass windows and radiant light shining in. When two people are dancing together, whether it is the Salsa, Waltz, Tango, Cha-Cha or Foxtrot, one person is leading, and one is following. They are holding each other in a proper dance frame, strongly connected to their physical bodies, and one subtle movement from the person leading can be felt by the person who is following. Typically, there is a great deal of trust involved for the person who is following, especially for dances like Tango where the "follower" is moving backward, not being able to see where they're going, and the "lead" is walking forwards. It takes time for both people to understand the lead and follow the process, to understand the music, and practice the steps. Once both people have practiced enough so that the dance steps become automatic and they can be in rhythm with each other and in rhythm with the music, then and only then, does the real magic happen. It becomes an almost indescribable experience of bliss, trust, flowing, and gliding around the room with grace and ease. The "letting go" that happens between two people who have chosen to surrender to the dance, to silently trust one another and cooperate with the established "lead and follow" agreement, is quite possibly one of the most freeing experiences on the planet.

I am inviting you to imagine this very same process with your understanding of the Divine (A.K.A. God, the Universe, Higher Self, the Creator, Source Energy, etc.). This process of letting go and melting into the arms of Divine guidance requires trust, relaxation and a state of surrender. You've got to know the steps of how to do this first though. You've got to know the steps and what it is that you desire in life. You've got to practice dancing with the Divine first so that you can learn the process of leading and following. It's not that you're just following what the Divine wants you to do. It's more like creating a life together as you move in rhythm together. It's about co-creation. It's about the Divine guiding you to lead a life connected to your heart's deepest desire. You find a way to move and flow with the Divine. When you become in alignment with the Divine and you begin to coincide together, the dance becomes graceful and effortless. The entire world will applaud as you and the Divine move together in complete unison with the music and rhythm of life.

And now you're probably asking… "HOW exactly do I do that?!"

CHAPTER 2:

BASIC STEPS – LEARNING TO TRUST INTUITION AND FOLLOW DIVINE GUIDANCE

Have you ever had one of those occasions where your intuition (a.k.a. your instincts or gut reaction) tells you to do something but that "something" defies all logic, sanity and original plans you had? Let's call this something "Option A" for the purpose of this description. This something could be a major life decision, a choice about your relationship or travel or work or school. And, if you're reading this book, you've probably been there. So, let's not forget the most challenging part! Then comes the part when you try to push your intuition or instincts down. You try to tuck them away in some dark place as you repeat the logical approach in your mind repeatedly to convince yourself that Option B is much more appropriate and suitable. Perhaps you talk to your friends about how Option B is best for you and everyone else involved. Maybe you journal about Option B or create a list of the Pros and Cons for Option A as well as the Pros and Cons of Option B. Then you're left with this state of confusion because no matter what you do, Option B just doesn't FEEL right. All the while, there's this lingering, nagging feeling, deep down inside, patiently, quietly waiting to be acknowledged. Intuition and instinct are simply smiling, or laughing, waiting for you to choose Option A because it's truly in your highest good and in perfect alignment with what your soul wants and what the Divine wants for you.

This is the part where it's important for your own personal growth, the growth of your soul and the spiritual growth of the planet, for you to follow your instincts and intuition. It is almost your duty, at this point of spiritual evolution on the planet, to follow your heart and instincts. Assuming you are one of the brave and enlightened ones who started on the spiritual path some time ago, it is almost a responsibility at this point to follow your intuition and your gut. Listening to your intuition, ignoring logic, forgetting about what others think, defying the odds and perhaps going against old conditioning or social norms is not always an easy task. This does require a certain level of confidence and bravery as well as a deep connection to your body as intuition is often felt deep at the gut level. It also requires a strong sense of self and simply knowing what's best and right for you. No one else can tell you…well, except for the Divine maybe. Most often it's Divine guidance that has led you to this place of making this decision or choice anyway.

This is one of the greatest lessons I have learned in my life thus far, although I'm sure the Divine is excited with anticipation to teach me more. At one point in my life, I was asked to make a major decision about a significant relationship. To move forward or to end the relationship was the question. I was asked if I was sure that I wanted to move forward with the relationship and deep down inside my body screamed "NO," but out of my mouth came the words "Yes, of course." It was almost like the screams of my body and intuition couldn't be heard because they were drowned out by the voices of logic, reason, and social expectations. At that point, I had also not yet developed or strengthened the pattern of listening to intuition. The next seven years of my life involved a lot of ups and downs, good times and challenging times, as well as frustration and trying to make things work. But you and I both also know that intuition can only be held in that dark, quiet place for so long. Although many lessons were learned along the way, and I would not necessarily go back and change anything, I can now say that intuition eventually came to the surface and lovingly guided me to end that relationship. Intuition came through loud and clear, like a marching band when it was time to leave. And thankfully I listened to it that time around.

At this point, you may be wondering now how to develop intuition or trust Divine guidance. What exactly does it feel like? How do I know when the Divine is guiding me? What if I get it wrong?

First things first, it's a bit of a confusing process to learn to trust your intuition and Divine guidance. Notice that I chose to use the word "learn". This is a learning process as described by the Four Stages of Competence Model in chapter one. As you begin to learn how to listen to your intuition, your mind will likely try to overpower it since you may have been living from that place for most of your life. In fact, when we first arrive on this planet as young children we are typically quite intuitive. Sometimes we are conditioned out of listening to our heart and intuition because our parents or teachers encourage us to follow the norms of society or what they think is best or right for us. They, of course, mean no harm and are only trying to help in the best way they know how. The good news is that sometimes learning to follow intuition is more a process of just remembering how we used to let it guide us.

The only way to start listening to this type of guidance is to go with it when you believe this is happening. Just take the leap because you cannot get it "wrong". It is a matter of trusting, allowing and then practicing as often as you can to strengthen that muscle of intuition. If you are worried about getting it "wrong" then start with something small as opposed to something life-changing. For example, start with intuitively choosing a meal from a menu. When you go to a restaurant and you have the menu in your hands, begin by closing your eyes, become quiet inside, relax your mind, ask your body what it needs right now for nourishment, then gently open your eyes and observe what pops out at you on the menu or which item appears to be highlighted for you. This was one of the ways I started to practice intuition. Items on the menu would almost jump off the page at me or appear bolder, glowing or emphasized. If I went with that choice I was always guaranteed to be satisfied with the meal.

The other way to practice developing intuition in a safe way before making more significant decisions is to walk into a crowded room of people and ask the Divine if there is anyone in the room that it would be beneficial for you to meet or interact with. Close your eyes for a moment, relax, ground yourself in your feet, feel yourself within your physical body and let the Divine guide you to who you need to meet. Open your eyes and look around the room with a clear mind and see who stands out for you. This person will be drawn to you like a magnet or vice versa. The important part is to relax, practice, experiment and have fun with it. Remember that the strengthening and trusting of intuition and Divine guidance comes with time.

To further clear up some confusion about learning to trust and follow intuition, let's examine the experience a little more:

Trusting intuition feels like this…

- Gut reaction or sense of knowing
- Subtle sensation or inkling in the body
- Third eye chakra pulsating
- Heart chakra opening
- A repetitive sense of being pulled or drawn in one direction
- Instant trust in the person, option or decision
- The "little voice" deep down inside
- Receiving signs from the Divine (the key is to ask for signs!)
- Relief once the right choice is made

Not trusting intuition feels like this…

- Ruminating in your mind
- Overthinking or overanalyzing

- Worrying
- Convincing self
- Unsettled sensation, usually in your gut
- Asking others for opinions
- An underlying nervous or anxious feeling
- Constant indecision
- Feeling incongruent with self

One of the most effective ways to develop your intuition is also to practice a Third Eye Meditation. The Third Eye Chakra or Anja Chakra is also known as the sixth sense and the center of intuition. This energy center is located in the middle of the forehead between the eyebrows and is closely associated with the pineal gland. When the energy of this chakra is balanced it allows for connection to our internal sense of knowing and the ability to receive non-verbal messages from the Divine. One of the recommended meditations for balancing the pineal gland and strengthening intuition is a Kundalini Yoga meditation called the "Kirtan Kriya" or the "Sa Ta Na Ma" meditation. The benefits of practicing the Kirtan Kriya include increasing intuitive abilities while clearing negative emotions, traumas, and impressions. The meditation also uplifts the emotional body, builds concentration, bestows peace and gives someone awareness of their Divine Infinite Nature. The meditation uses the power of visualization to activate the higher chakras and associated endocrine glands. Specifically, this mantra meditation is going to activate the Crown Chakra and the Ajna Chakra (Third Eye), thus it will stimulate the pineal and pituitary glands respectively. It is recommended that this meditation is practiced specifically as described by Yogi Bhajan and can be found online. Beginning with a consistent 40-day practice for 11 minutes or 31 minutes a day of this meditation is a healthy way to transition into living by intuition and allowing yourself to be guided by the Divine. In the practice of Kundalini Yoga, the timing of meditations and kriyas has great significance. Three minutes: Affects your circulation, blood chemistry and stability of the blood. The increased blood circulations begin distributing enhanced neuroendocrine secretions throughout the body. Seven minutes: Brain patterns start to shift from the static of beta waves to calmer alpha waves and ultimately into deep relaxing delta waves. Simultaneously, the magnetic force surrounding the body increases in strength. Eleven minutes: The pituitary gland, glandular system, and the nerves start to learn and change. The sympathetic and parasympathetic nervous systems begin to accommodate increased energy. Thirty-one minutes: Affects your whole mind and your aura. Endocrine balance is achieved, as is a balance of the chakras of the ethereal body. This balance persists throughout the day and is reflected by changes in moods and behavior. The more you practice the Third Eye Meditation and use your intuition, the stronger it becomes. Eventually, you move into a state of being "unconsciously competent" when it comes to trusting your intuition. This means that it becomes your natural way of being or more automatic for you to trust your instincts instead of overthinking choices.

My personal experience of trusting intuition and Divine guidance, after much practice, has become very powerful and magical. There came a day when I asked for help and guidance because I felt very lost, unsure and indecisive. At the time, I was in a pattern of being indecisive over menial things even, like what to buy when doing groceries. I experienced frustration and anxiety more often than I experienced bliss, joy, and connectedness. The moment I asked for help and was truly in a place of letting go and willing to receive that help, I was blessed with Divine guidance. Quite literally, it felt like the Divine picked me up, held my hand, wrapped its arms around me and said, "Come with me…I will show you the way." Keep in mind that the Divine does not speak in actual words like you or I might have a conversation. There is an understanding and a transfer of information. There is a feeling or sense of "Come with me…I will show you the way," layered with love and trust. At times there are images that appear in my mind of where to go or what to do next. The image typically appears in the area of the Third Eye Chakra, as mentioned. Other times, the Divine is completely merged and amplified within my physical body as though it takes over the steering wheel and directs me where to go. The Divine indicates which direction for me to go in by providing a stronger sensation on my right or left side. I then know which way to turn or look. The energy of the Divine will also slightly pull me forward or back at times. The direction provided is always safe and secure although sometimes stronger than others. Most often it almost feels like a loving, nurturing parent leading me where I need to go or showing me what I need to see in order to provide me with a message.

Like following a leader on the dance floor, sometimes the lead is stronger than others. When one is first learning to dance and following the partner who is leading on the dance floor, because our ability to pick up subtle cues or body movements is not yet developed, the leader must be strong, powerful, clear and direct with their lead. As the dance becomes more automatic and you become better at following the partner who is leading on the dance floor, the lead becomes more and more subtle. The lead can be soft, simple, and delicate and, because the brain and the body have become accustomed to the dance, it's easy to respond quickly and precisely. You will know exactly where to go and when, and with exact timing to the music. This is when the magic happens! The Divine sometimes would lead me like I was a beginner and would be strong and powerful but, as I developed the skill of dancing with the Divine, it became easier and easier to follow more and more subtle cues, hints and guidance.

In order to understand how this process of being guided by the Divine unfolds for most people, it's important to first describe just how deep our connection is with the Divine. Unfortunately, there truly are no words that can accurately describe this connection. The essence of it is lost simply by trying to put it into words since the depth is unfathomable. Once you experience this connection in your heart you will without a doubt, find yourself longing to connect as often as possible. The Divine knows everything about you. It's very important to understand the depth of this statement. The Divine knows absolutely everything about you. By that, I mean it hears every word you say, every thought you think, every feeling you have, and every wish, worry, hope, and secret. It knows you more intimately than you can possibly imagine, and yes, still loves you unconditionally knowing all of this about you. It is always present, everywhere and in everything. There is no time at which the Divine ever leaves your side; there are only times when we are disconnected from it. The Divine loves you fully, completely and unconditionally. The Divine only longs to connect with you and to guide you to experience joy, happiness, and peace on all levels. The Divine is not separate from you in any way. It never has been and never will be.

The most beautiful part is that every living being on the planet has the potential to live this way and connect with this Divine Universal energy. My deepest desire is that you learn from my experiences of interacting with the Divine so that you can enjoy this blissful, magical state as well. There have been a number of occasions when I have been blessed with Divine Guidance that left me thinking... "How did you know that? No, seriously. HOW did you know that?" There have been instances where I had thoughts about needing something, and had not told another living soul, had not written it down, and not said it out loud. That same day the Divine would pick me up or nudge me and guide me to the place, person or thing that I had been thinking about earlier that day. There's no other way to describe it except that the energy of the Divine seems to amplify within my body and become my GPS or guidance system temporarily leading me in a specific direction.

Initially, the Divine guidance started with small things, which makes sense looking back now as it takes time to develop trust. I would be guided to go to a huge department store, that I had never been in before, and be guided to just the right place, to find just the right item that I had been thinking of buying earlier as a birthday gift for a friend. It often feels like being drawn like a magnet to exactly what I have in mind. The process of finding things in large department stores became easy and effortless where before I had learned to connect with the Divine, I would often wander around places as such, aimlessly with frustration not being able to find what I was looking for. Other times I would be thinking of a remedy that I would need from a health food store but neglect to go purchase. Then, while I was out driving the Divine would sneak up on me and whisper "this way", and I would acquiesce, almost like allowing the Divine to take over the steering wheel of my car. "Turn here" the Divine would whisper, and I would allow myself to be led. Then the arms of the Divine would support me and walk me right into the Health food store and bring me to a halt in the most appropriate aisle. I would find myself standing in front of the very product that my body needed and that I was thinking of earlier. This is usually the point when I smile at the Divine and say thank you for reminding me to take care of my body.

In addition to the Divine hearing every thought you have, being omniscient and omnipresent, it has great love and compassion as well as a sweet sense of humor. At times in the past, I had thought about my desire to leave my office job and become self-employed full time instead. I would be speaking with a co-worker about this vision and desire that I had. On my way home from work the Divine would encourage me and steer me into a local shopping mall and guide me over to a store that had a section of greeting cards. And then I would be steered directly in front of the section of cards that would say "Congratulations on your New Job". I would just laugh and smile at the Divine and silently say thank you as I knew with all my heart that if the Divine heard my wishes and guided me there to show me that card then it could certainly guide me to the right people, places, and situations in my life that would be required for me to become self-employed full-time and leave my job. The Divine also entertained me using a cute sense of humor and compassion another time when I wasn't feeling well one day. I could feel myself coming down with a cold or flu and knew that others around me had been sick lately. As I decided to take care of myself and take the rest of the day off work, I stopped at a local grocery store on the way home to pick up some soup. After filling my shopping cart with the few items I needed, the Divine guided me over to the greeting card section again. This time, I was drawn like a magnet to a section where all I could see was the "Get Well" cards as they stood out like a neon sign. What a sweet message to receive and such a creative way to provide me with a message. For a long time, whenever the Divine wanted to communicate with me or provide me with a message, it would guide me to a book store or magazine rack or section of greeting cards and the message would always be highlighted for me. Most of the time the message would reflect thoughts I had been thinking or a conversation I had earlier that day.

This all-knowing Divine Spirit has also guided me during times of travel to foreign places. In the summer of 2013, I traveled for my first time to British Columbia and Alberta. While staying in Banff, Alberta for a few nights, I was very much looking forward to trying new restaurants. Earlier during the day, I had seen advertisements for an Indian restaurant called Masala and a healthy place called Nourish Bistro, both of which were located in the downtown core of Banff. Feeling hungry that evening, I left my hotel, hopped in my car, headed into town and later realized that I had forgotten my map. I had no idea where these restaurants were. I had decided that I wanted to find the Nourish Bistro and asked the Divine to simply help guide me there. I could feel the presence of the Divine with me at that time, quietly asking me to open my eyes and pay attention. I was sitting at a stop sign when I noticed the truck in front of me had the logo of the Masala restaurant on the back of it. The truck was turning left at the stop sign and the Divine nudged me to follow the truck. I remembered that the two restaurants were relatively close to each other in location. The truck sped up and I noticed a car on the right side of the road pulling out of a parking spot. I slowed down, allowing the car to pull out in front of me. The Divine encouraged me to take that same parking spot and so I did. As I stepped out of my car, unbeknownst to me, I parked right in front of Nourish Bistro. I attempted to put some money in the parking meter but that was not necessary either because the previous driver had left over an hour of paid time in the meter. Feeling grateful and laughing inside, I let the Divine know how much I appreciated the guidance and headed into Nourish to enjoy the most fabulous meal with a smile on my face.

I have also been blessed with the opportunity to realize that the Divine has a very gentle and loving approach to help us overcome things from our past that we may feel embarrassed about. For several reasons, I grew up in a home where I never learned to cook. Old stereotypes and social conditioning I received gave me the message that a woman should know and be able to cook delicious, well-balanced meals at home for their family. True or not, that was my perception growing up. So, by the time I was in my thirties and recognized that I had yet to develop this incredibly important skill, I had attached a certain feeling of embarrassment to the fact that I was very much lacking in the kitchen skills department. The Divine was aware of this fact and my desire to learn how to cook as I started to come to terms with this. I told no one about this desire and only contemplated in my mind once or twice about the possibility of taking a cooking class.

A few weeks later, after finishing work late, I found myself debating what to do with the rest of my evening. Perhaps the gym or yoga class or just to head home. I wanted to head to a yoga class but when I looked at the clock, I realized I might be late. The Divine decided promptly to intervene with the chronic indecision about what to do and instead showed me an image in my mind of the local Chapters bookstore. And I replied, "Really...right now?" This is when the Divine just smiled at me and waited patiently as I can feel it in my heart. "Fine, let's go" I answered. The Divine sweetly and softly supported me on the drive there. When we arrived in the parking lot the Divine swept me up into its arms, guided me into the bookstore and even though I have no idea what I was doing there I somehow know exactly where to go. We promptly stopped in the cookbook section and I just happened to be standing in front of a copy of Jessica Seinfeld's book called "The Can't Cook Book: Recipes for the Absolutely Terrified". The book, of course, provides very clear instructions in a nonjudgmental way for total beginners. What a wonderful way to end kitchen phobia! My years of embarrassment and shame about not being able to cook began to dissolve into tears and dripped onto the carpet of the bookstore in that very moment. "How did you know Divine? How did you know that I really want to learn to cook but don't have a clue where to start? How did you know this book was here? And that it would be the perfect book for me?" The answer was clear. And without any words, I came to a deeper understanding that the Divine truly is omniscient and omnipresent. I felt the Divine simply smile at me with pure love and affection as I wandered over to the counter to purchase the book.

After having such experiences of dancing with the Divine and allowing myself to be led by my intuition, I decided that from this point forward, I would trust the Divine completely. I would let the Divine lead me. Every time I felt the nudge from the Divine, I would respond. Whether the lead was subtle or strong I would practice the art of following. I would question less, force less and try less. I would allow more, relax more and trust more. And let the magic unfold....

Should you so choose to begin to live your life in a way that feels like you are supported in the arms of the Divine every day, here are the specific dance steps to trusting Divine Guidance:

Step One: Practice the Kirtan Kriya (Kundalini Meditation) or meditate on the Third Eye

Step Two: Ask the Divine for Guidance When Needed

Step Three: Allow the Mind to Be Quiet and the Body Relaxed

Step Four: Follow Guidance without Judgment

Let's elaborate, shall we?

Step One:
Practice the Kirtan Kriya (Kundalini Meditation) or meditate on the Third Eye

Strengthening your intuition via these meditation practices will make it easier to work with Divine Guidance. The Kirtan Kriya can be found easily on many websites online, however, the most appropriate source of information would be www.3ho.org so that you can learn the practice as it was originally taught by Yogi Bhajan himself. This powerful meditation not only strengthens your intuition and connection to the Divine, but it cleanses the subconscious mind and balances the hemispheres of the brain. The gaze or focus point will be at your third eye during this process which is important. It is recommended that you commit to a 40-day practice when you first begin so that you can establish the new pattern and new vibration in your energy field around you. Why 40 days you ask? Yogi Bhajan explained that it takes 40 days to break a habit, 90 days to gain the new habit, 120 days and you are the new habit, 1,000 days you are the Master of it. As mentioned before, this is a process. A process of rolling a new snowball and continuing to roll that snowball until you are a master at it. When you stay focused on the new snowball (or a new way of being, or new vibration), your old snowball (or way of being, or new vibration) eventually begins to melt away. This means that the more you practice using your intuition and strengthen your intuition via meditation, the more powerful your intuition becomes. And the more intuitive you become, the more intuitive you become. And the closer you get to the Divine, the closer you get to the Divine. So, do your best to commit yourself to 40 days simply because you love yourself enough to make this change and because you're worth it.

The practice can be a variety of different lengths: 11 minutes, 31 minutes, 1 hour or 2 ½ hours. Please choose a length of time that you know you can fit into your schedule easily every day, for the next 40 days. It is also recommended that you adhere to the meditation practice as described without making any modifications to it. Like a very specific and precious recipe, from an important lineage in your family, it is best enjoyed and most effective when it is respected and practiced as it has been passed down. And enjoy the process! Your attitude with which you approach the practice is just as important too. Instead of viewing it as something you "have" to do, see it as your special time to take care of you. If you have questions about the Kriya it is relatively easy and highly recommended to find a Kundalini Yoga Teacher within your community by going to www.ikyta.org. If you truly desire to develop your intuition and deepen your connection with the Divine, it would be recommended that instead of just doing the meditation you instead engage in a full Kundalini practice or classes on a weekly basis. This means you would be rolling the snowball a little faster!

If you do not feel that you are drawn to practice the Kirtan Kriya you can simply practice a different Third Eye or Anja Chakra meditation. This center of intuition can be awakened by focusing all of our awareness and attention there. Find a quiet place with no distractions, sit tall with your spine lengthened, begin by following the rhythmic flow of your breath, and allow thoughts to simply fall away without being attached to them. Once the mind becomes quiet, place your attention on the middle of the forehead, between the eyebrows. Imagine the third eye center beginning to soften and the breath flowing freely in and out from this space. If you prefer, you can imagine a bright white light radiating out from the third eye as you keep your focus here. Start by practicing daily for 10 minutes and lengthen the meditation if you are comfortable with the process. If you choose to practice a third eye meditation, please remember to also practice other chakra meditations to keep balanced and stay grounded as well. Opening the Third Eye can lead to feeling more connected to the Divine, having stronger intuition and psychic experiences.

It is also recommended that you seek out a qualified yoga teacher or meditation teacher in your community to guide you through this practice. If you feel overwhelmed by the experience, spend time meditating on the lower three chakras (Root Chakra, Sacral Chakra, and Solar Plexus Chakra) to have a more integrated experience.

Step Two:
Ask the Divine for Guidance When Needed

Although most of my initial experiences of being guided by the Divine happened without me asking, I have since learned that all I need to do now is ask for help when I do need guidance. We all know it's in our best interest to ask for help when it's needed. However, sometimes, for some reason, we fail to do so. Perhaps we've been conditioned out of asking for help as we've just become used to doing everything ourselves or resolving a solution in the best way that we know how. To live a more fulfilling life, and a life that is more coherent with our soul's yearnings, we sometimes have to ask the Ego to step aside and allow something greater to step in. The Divine is actually patiently waiting at all times and willing to help you. The best part is that the Divine is actually able to provide you with options or a solution that is beyond what you could possibly imagine. If you're resolving an issue or problem in your life on your own, chances are you are choosing a way to do so that worked for you in the past. Unless you're consciously choosing to resolve the issue in a new and creative way, you are likely to operate from a past pattern and therefore experience similar outcomes in your life. If you are currently extremely happy with the outcomes in your life, then keep doing what you're doing. However, if your heart and soul know deeply that there is a more profound way to experience life and you feel stuck, then you must ask for help. Trust and know that the Divine always has the best of intentions for you to achieve your heart's deepest desires and knows the best way for you to get there.

Should you choose to ask the Divine to dance and provide you with guidance and help, you must be open to the issue or problem being resolved in a completely different way than you might have imagined. In fact, that's the whole point. The idea when you ask the Divine for help is to get out of your own way, allowing a completely different solution to find you or for you to find it, in the most effortless way. This means giving up control of the outcome. This can be the most challenging part and sometimes even scary for those who are typically comfortable in a leadership role themselves. Oddly enough, the part where we get to relax and allow the Divine to take over the "solution steering wheel" can also be one of the most gratifying, amusing, and joyous experiences.

Remember as well that, sometimes, the Divine needs to show you just one step at a time when you ask for help in order to guide you to the ultimate solution. Take note that the first steps provided might not make sense, at least initially. The most important part is to trust and go along for the dance, one step at a time, and a way will be shown to you that was just outside of your current state of awareness or that you never even thought possible.

How exactly do you ask for help? There is no right or wrong way to ask for help. Avoid getting caught up in the details of what to specifically say. It can be as simple as saying "Please help me." You can ask more specifically by saying "Please help me resolve this situation" or "Please help me find what I'm looking for." Another more reverent way to ask for help might sound like this...

"Dear Divine Universe, will you dance with me? Will you please help me with this situation? Will you guide me with your infinite wisdom, love, and grace to resolve this situation in a more perfect way for me than I could possibly imagine. I invite your blessed presence to lead me to the most flawless solution. May we move together with grace and ease towards the most magical answer to this problem. My heart and mind are open to receiving your guidance in the infinitely creative way that only you can provide. Thank you, thank you, thank you. I am eternally grateful for your help and guidance."

You can say this out loud or silently in your mind. You need only to say it once however if you feel inclined to ask again, feel free to do so as long as it does not come from a place of worry. It is important to trust that the Divine will guide you when the time is right. And then, of course, let go of your attachment to the outcome because the solution or steps to take may not look like anything of which you had previously conceived. The relaxing and letting go part is most essential to this process. If you have uncertainty about this process and are not used to asking for help, then it is best to start with asking for help with something that you believe to be small like finding something in a store or in your home. Once you experience starting to follow your intuition and Divine guidance, you will become more confident and trusting of the Divine and willing to ask more often.

Step Three:
Allow the Mind to Be Quiet and the Body Relaxed

When you feel the inkling of intuition or the nudge of Divine guidance attempting to lead you in a certain direction, this is the time to listen. Turn down the television or radio or any noise in your environment if you can. Place your awareness in your feet and notice where you are in the present moment. Simply notice your surroundings with your eyes wide open. Then, follow a long deep full breath in and a long deep full breath out and repeat and repeat. Stay grounded in your physical body, allow any unnecessary thoughts to simply pass by and settle your energy by repeating the word "relax" in your mind. Open yourself up to listen to Divine guidance. You can listen not only with your ears but also with your eyes or your entire body. When the mind is quiet, it is easier to listen to the body and typically intuition or Divine guidance is a felt sense or experience in the body.

Remember that the Divine is omnipotent, omnipresent and omniscient. Perhaps you have not asked for help with something specifically as mentioned in Step Two but instead, you've been thinking about something you need or desire in your life lately. The Divine knows of this silent asking and at times, unexpectedly will pick you up and guide you to show you what you've been thinking about. If your mind is busy and distracted or you are not tuned into your physical body, it is possible that you may miss the inkling of intuition or nudge of Divine presence. When the body is relaxed, and the mind is quiet you will be able to follow the guidance which can come in different forms for different people.

You may feel the amplification of energy in your entire body or like a Divine Spirit is merging fully with you and taking over the steering wheel. Quite literally, the Divine will physically pull you or guide you where to go in your current environment, in a loving and gentle way of course. You simply need to pay attention to your physical body at this time, relax, let go and follow. Sometimes, if you pay attention to what you see in your environment, someone or something will stand out for you, as if it is being highlighted or your focus will be drawn to them. Otherwise, if you listen carefully, you might be able to hear the Divine whispers of what to do or where to go next.

This guidance can come immediately after asking the Divine for help or it may come days, weeks, months or even years later. This is where patience and trust come into play. It depends on what you're asking for, if what you're asking for is anywhere near your current environment, how many steps might be involved in guiding you to what you're asking for and if you're currently vibrating and resonating at a level that allows you to bring that person or experience into your life. Sometimes the guidance can even come at an "inconvenient" time. For example, the Divine may want to show you something or provide you with a message when you're in the middle of brushing your teeth. Just go with it. It'll all make sense…. eventually.

Step Four:
Follow Guidance without Judgment

So, this is what the experience of following the Divine may sound like in your mind and simultaneously feel like in your body. There will be an initial awareness of Divine presence and all you need to do is relax and decide you're ready to dance. Let go, allowing yourself to be led and give your body permission to follow. Consciously stay in the present moment so that you may follow one step at a time to receive the message or sign that the Divine wants to provide you with. Avoid questioning, judging or making assumptions about what the message is or where you are going. Simply remain open to the experience because in this moment there are infinite possibilities.

And like being led on a dance floor you will feel as though the Divine is asking you if you're ready to listen with your body and your mind. The Divine will indicate to you via subtle guidance to follow along. Go right. Move forward down the hall. Go left. Go to the other side of the table. Stop. No. A little further. Good. Look down. Right there in front of you. Look a little closer.

And there they are…the earrings you thought you lost forever that you just happened to be thinking about this morning. Just smile or laugh and extend your deepest gratitude to the Divine at this point.

There may also be occasions when you don't understand, or you become confused by what the Divine is trying to tell you. You can develop, with practice, the ability to ask and "check in" with the Divine to confirm that you're picking up the message that is being conveyed to you. Perhaps you will experience a pullback or leaning back of your physical body when the answer is "No" or a gentle leaning forward when the answer is "Yes". It is up to you and the Divine to learn to communicate and to lead and follow in this way. It will almost be like coming up with your own language. You may hear what the Divine must tell you or see images or have a sensory experience where you feel the guidance in your body, or a combination of all these methods. What is most important is that you practice as often as you can to develop the skill.

At times you may be guided to someone or something and think, "Really? Are you sure?" as it may not seem to fit with what you've been thinking about. Again, as you suspend judgment about the potential of the experience with that person, place or thing, you will more than likely be pleasantly surprised with what the Divine has creatively come up with for you!

Practice makes perfect as we all know so continue to practice and repeat these steps as often as you can and just observe how the guidance and communication become clearer and the connection becomes stronger. And as you continue to practice you will also begin to experience more synchronicities, magic, and miracles in your life!

CHAPTER 3:

INTERMEDIATE STEPS – SYNCHRONICITY, MAGIC, AND MIRACLES

When you are living in flow and dancing effortlessly with the Divine, your life can become magical. One way of knowing that you're living this way is that you will consistently experience synchronicities and moments that feel like life is unfolding in a magical way that you couldn't possibly have planned it better yourself. Synchronistic events are moments of coincidences that have a deeper meaning for the soul. Synchronicity can also be described as the effortless unfolding of events that seem exquisitely connected and that happen in perfect Divine timing. You've likely experienced a synchronistic event in your life before and were left with a sense of awe, wonderment or amazement. Perhaps laughter was involved too as the Divine can have a great sense of humor sometimes! You know…when you spend some time thinking of good old times that you had with a friend that happens to live on the other side of the world now, and you have not spoken to each other in over a year and then the next day you get a phone call or email from them. Or that time when you've got a random song stuck in your head that you haven't heard in a while and then you turn on the radio and there it is. And that other time when you were thinking about looking something up in a book, but you can't find it on your bookshelf and then your co-worker happens to bring the exact same book into the office the next day. Really, there is an infinite number of situations that may have happened in life that left you saying to yourself, "I was JUST thinking about that!" or "Wow, what perfect timing!" which is better known as a synchronistic event or coincidence.

So how exactly do synchronistic events happen then? One way of understanding such events is to imagine an enormous spider web. Picture a spider web that is very intricate, delicate, and has a sophisticated pattern. This complex and iridescent web sparkles when the sun shines on it. Of course, there is also a spider that has produced this web. Now, spiders have a very keen sense of touch. Spiders learn much more about the world around them by feeling vibrations on their web than they learn from using their eyes. They can tell what is happening around them by feeling the differences between different vibrations, such as the wind blowing through their web vs. a fly landing on their web. Imagine for a moment that a fly lands in this enormous spider web and the vibration is felt far off in the distance where the spider is quietly waiting. The spider then simply responds to the vibration that they feel in a way that only nature knows how to do. Now, this Universe that we live in is actually very similar to this spider web, however, the web we live in is more like a spider web sphere or ball of a spider web, where everyone and everything is connected. The iridescent sparkle within the web, in this case, is the Divine that is woven throughout the sphere or ball. All things are intricately connected within this web and so you are not separate from anyone or anything. This means that when you are thinking of your friend that lives in Australia that you haven't seen in a year, it's like tugging on one string of the spider web. Your friend is of course also connected to this web and just like the spider which is why they feel the vibration of your thoughts at an unconscious level. This web is also known as the "collective unconscious". As your friend receives your thoughts at an unconscious level it prompts them to also think thoughts of you and causes them to initiate contact via phone or email. Sometimes it becomes a more of a "what comes first, the chicken or the egg" type of debate. Was it your thought that triggered them or were they thinking of you first? And sometimes, it happens simultaneously and immediately when you are thinking of each other at the same time and then call or text each other at the same moment. Again, this is simply a reflection of the divinely organized, beautifully created, and intricate web of the collective unconscious.

Once you begin to become more tuned in with the Divine and this web you will typically begin to experience more and more synchronistic events in your life. As I became interested in synchronistic events and noticed that they were beginning to happen in my life I decided to start a little experiment. I decided to start writing in a "Synchronicity Journal". At that time, I had heard about the importance of writing a Gratitude Journal and focusing our attention on what we are grateful for in our lives. The purpose, of course, was so that one could draw into their life and experience more things to be grateful for. I loved experiencing little miracles and synchronistic events in my life so much that I wanted to experience them every day, all day. Hence, the purpose of writing down every synchronistic event in my journal as often as possible! My friends and family probably got a little exhausted of me or thought I was a bit bizarre, but I didn't care. I was absolutely overjoyed and ecstatic every single time something magical happened that I would tell as many people as possible and then make sure to write it down in my Synchronicity Journal at the end of the day. Sometimes it was just a relatively small event like thinking of a friend and then that friend would call and invite me to lunch. Other times it was a significant event like desiring extra money to attend a potentially life-changing conference and the money manifesting from an unexpected source within days of me signing up for it. Within six months I had experienced over two hundred synchronistic events and my journal was filling up with magical and miraculous synchronistic events faster than I could have imagined. By that point, experiencing events as such was simply a way of life for me. It was as if the more I focused on synchronicities in my life the more that they were provided for me. The art and dance of this practice is a delicate one as it simultaneously requires you to get out of your own way, let go and allow the events to unfold in their own way. The best part is the feeling of surprise or amazement that arises when this happens. That feeling, at least for me, is priceless, because I know and recognize that at the moment the Divine is with me and within me.

And so, for your inspiration and to strengthen your belief in the powerful ability for the Divine to arrange coincidences, here are some of the most entertaining moments of synchronicity that I experienced while keeping my Synchronicity Journal...

1) This synchronistic event really made me laugh and realize just how perfect Divine timing can be. I had been feeling sick for a day or so and knew that I needed to see a doctor. As I was driving along in my car, I looked at the clock and realized that my doctor's office was now closed for the weekend. Since I was leaving for a trip early the next week it was important for me to see a doctor before I left. Feeling a little worried, I started to think about where I could go. I started to wonder about whether the new Walk-In Medical Clinic would still be open at this time. I figured I could just drive over to the medical clinic to see if they were open as it would only take fifteen minutes or so. Since I had other errands to run still, I decided it would be easier to call instead of driving over there, although I didn't have the phone number. So, I called home to ask a family member to look up the clinic phone number and information for me so that I would know what time they were open until. As I'm on the phone with the family member, I confirm the name of the Clinic and the location as they are searching for the phone number on the internet. Oddly enough, they're having trouble finding the phone number on the internet.

Patiently waiting and hoping, I'm still driving around, while on the phone, waiting to see if they're able to find the number for me. I stop at the next red light and the sound of the brakes on the bus in front of me catches my attention. As I look at the advertisement on the back of the bus, I actually burst out laughing. My family member, still on the phone with me, searching the internet unsuccessfully, asks me what I'm laughing at. I proceed to tell him that he no longer needs to search for the phone number because now, right in front of me is an advertisement on the back of the bus for the new Medical Walk-In Clinic! The phone number for the clinic is clearly, boldly printed on the back of the bus as well as the address and the hours of operation. And yes, the clinic was still open at that moment. The timing of the bus advertisement was impeccable! Laughing together, my family member and I decided to get off the phone and I continued to drive over to the clinic in a state of wonderment and feeling grateful for the infinite wisdom and magical timing of the Divine. In my heart and in every fiber of my being, I have complete trust at this point that the Divine was watching over me and felt my desire to seek medical attention before leaving on my trip and even though, I did not ask for help, the Divine was there in synchronistic timing to guide me in the right direction at just the right time.

2) This next synchronistic event was one that allowed me to realize the importance of letting go of expectations, trusting the Divine and to allow things to simply unfold as they may. It was originally, an average Tuesday morning at the office, checking email and Facebook while waiting for a client. I noticed on Facebook that my friend Natalie posted that she was going to attend and volunteer at an "Abraham-Hicks" Law of Attraction workshop in Toronto in about a month. Her post was asking if anyone wanted to join her for free and

volunteer with her as there were a few spots available still. My body and heart said "Absolutely, yes!" and so I responded to her as soon as possible but by the time I did, she said all the remaining volunteer spots were taken. Much to my disappointment, I contemplated what to do as it was a great opportunity to see Abraham-Hicks while they were in Toronto.

I decided to head over to the other side of the office to speak to my colleague Victoria about the workshop as I knew she would possibly be interested in attending and purchasing tickets instead. Now, normally I would take the most direct way to my colleague's desk, however, something told me for some reason, to take the other way around today. As I took a slight detour instead of walking straight to the other office I "just happened" to notice a poster on the wall, which I had probably walked by hundreds of times and never noticed. The poster seemed highlighted and really stood out for me. It simply read "Tell Us If You Are Volunteering!" with an image of helping hands. Now, the poster was really meant for clients to tell their counselors if they were involved with a volunteer opportunity but as soon as I noticed it, I simply laughed inside and quietly said to the Divine "Yes, I would like to volunteer at the Abraham-Hicks workshop please!" After speaking with my colleague Victoria about the workshop we decided to just think about it and decide later since it was still over a month away.

When I went back to my desk I opened my calendar book and flipped to the date of the Saturday workshop and wrote in big, bold letters "Volunteering at Abraham-Hicks Workshop", even though at that moment, Natalie had told me there was no way that would happen and I had no idea how exactly that was going to happen. I closed my calendar book, went on with my day at the office and made a conscious choice to let go. When I say I let go, I mean that I trusted whole heartedly that I would be there volunteering that day and stopped thinking about the event. I didn't worry or wonder or even ask Natalie about the workshop again. Approximately six weeks later, I was home on a Friday night and a little voice told me to check my calendar as I was wondering about plans for the weekend. As I opened my calendar book, I was almost surprised to realize that the Abraham-Hicks event was the following morning and I had totally forgotten about it! There was my note to myself about volunteering for the event, looking like everything else I schedule in my book, staring back at me. My feeling was one of total surrender and my only thought was actually "Oh, well". I headed off to bed with plans to relax and sleep in the next morning.

Those plans changed abruptly as the phone promptly rang at 8:30 am to wake me. It was Natalie calling from the workshop in Toronto in a bit of a panic. She explained that her friend that was supposed to be joining her to volunteer was sick that morning and decided last minute not to go! She wanted to know if I could make it to Toronto for 10:15 am as that was the allotted time for a break and she could bring me in at that time as a volunteer for the rest of the day. "Definitely, I will be there!" I told her and jumped out of bed to get ready as fast as I could since I needed at least an hour to drive there. I was grinning ear to ear the whole drive there, smiling at the convenient, synchronistic timing of the Divine. At the same time reminding myself that sometimes letting go of how things unfold and trusting the Divine can lead to outcomes better than we could imagine. As I walked into the auditorium at 10:30 am after the break, I could feel the presence of Abraham, radiating through Ester Hicks and I waited patiently for the audience to ask questions so that Abraham could share life lessons on manifesting and the law of attraction. And coincidently, the next two questions asked of Abraham were the only two questions I would have asked if I had been given the opportunity to speak with Abraham. One question was related to finding work that fills your heart and the other question was related to manifesting opportunities to travel. What a blessing, so conveniently arranged by the Divine, to spend the day with friends volunteering and to have my questions for Abraham asked indirectly, in perfect timing, so that I could leave with answers that I came for. This experience truly reaffirmed my belief in synchronistic events and the importance of letting go and allowing the Divine to arrange things!

3) This synchronistic event was a simple yet powerful and perfect example of what happens when our vibration is aligned with our desires. At that time in my career, I was thinking about my desire to work for Brock University in St. Catharines, Ontario. I was on the university website in the morning, scrolling through current career opportunities listed with Human Resources to work and teach there. Unfortunately, I did not find a position listed that I felt would be a good fit for

me so decided to click off the website and simply go about my day. A friend of mine had been working for the Continuing Education Program at the University for a few years at this point but I had not had contact with her in about six months. I had not even thought about contacting her to ask if she was aware of any internal positions posted that would be coming up soon. And I didn't need to contact her because later that day she emailed, in perfect synchronistic timing, to ask me if I would be interested in developing a course to teach for the Brock Continuing Education program in the coming winter. Smiling, feeling grateful for the Divine and totally in a state of flow, I replied to the email saying "Absolutely, yes." I wondered, to myself, "Can my whole life be like this? Can I live in this state of flow and connection to the Divine all the time?" Maybe, just maybe!

4) This next synchronistic event helps one to understand that even though we may not be consciously, directly asking the Divine for help or assistance we are, in fact, constantly asking via our thoughts and what we are focusing on. And sometimes when we get out of the way, the help we needed is provided. My family member and I were staying at a friend's chalet in Ellicottville, NY for a long weekend and felt very grateful for the opportunity to get away. The chalet was located on a lovely piece of property, with a wonderful hot tub out front for soaking the tension away. We talked about enjoying the hot tub later that day and my family member said we should probably balance the water with the chemicals it needs before we get in it, although, neither of us considered ourselves to be experts on how to do so. In fact, we had no idea how to do so

or where to find the proper chemicals and water testing kit. We decided to just relax instead and a few hours later as we were sitting outside, enjoying the sun, a man walked onto the property and introduced himself as the man who built the chalet and explained that he was friends with the owners as well. He explained that he comes by occasionally, on behalf of his friends to check on the condition of the hot tub and to ensure the chemicals are balanced so the hot tub can be used. He had with him, in his hands, everything he needed to do so and asked if we would mind him working on the hot tub for the next twenty minutes or so. We start laughing and tell him that we were thinking about balancing the hot tub chemicals a few hours ago and that we would be grateful for his efforts to do so and his expertise. It was almost as if this man randomly appeared out of nowhere to help us at just the perfect time. It was as though the Divine was aware of our quiet request for help via our conversation. The important part was the fact that we did not spend one moment worrying about "how" we could fix the hot tub or "when" we would do that. We simply spoke about it, let go, and even without awareness, allowed the Divine to arrange the perfect solution at the perfect time.

5) This simple synchronistic example is one that provides us with evidence that the Divine is always with us, in all places and always listening to our desires and thoughts. After arriving at an all-inclusive resort in Mexico for a week vacation, I took the time to explore the activities schedule as I often enjoy working out while away, almost as much as I enjoy eating all the fabulous food. It is of course, easy to lose track of time while on vacation as we can be simply in the moment enjoying

ourselves and typically I do not wear a watch anyway. So, on my first morning at the resort, I'm wandering around, exploring and trying to get a sense of where everything is located. I remembered from looking at the activities schedule the night before that there was a stretch class that was supposed to be happening on the beach that morning but not aware of the time or location of the class. I stopped to use the bathroom by the pool and as I was leaving the bathroom a woman walked by me who appears to be staff at the resort and I decided to ask her what time it was. She told me that it's 9:45 am and excitedly explains to me that there is a stretch class starting on the beach at 10 am that I was welcome to join. She just happened to be the instructor for the class! I smile and tell her I would love to join as she proceeds to politely guide me to the exact location. I didn't have to worry about the time or the location as I was simply guided in the right direction and finding the instructor for the class was absolutely a wonderful synchronistic moment for me.

6) Sometimes synchronistic events can happen when we ask the Divine for help with a certain situation and simply trust that the answer will be provided for us. At one time in my career, I was working part-time as a counselor in a large office setting and self-employed part-time as an Emotional Freedom Technique (E.F.T.) Practitioner and Trainer. After planning to host an E.F.T. Workshop, many of the fellow counselors at the office expressed interest in attending to learn about the technique. One morning about two weeks before the workshop, one of the fellow counselors approached me and handed me a cash deposit to secure her spot in the workshop,

however, she assumed that I knew her name and dashed off before I could confirm her name and contact information to register her. I spend the rest of the day thinking about who I could ask in the office to confirm who she was or how I could find her again to register her appropriately. I decided not to worry about it but rather ask the Divine to help me find a way to get the information I needed. The next morning, I had an unexpected visit from a fellow colleague and we were sitting in my office catching up when the same woman came by again. She greeted both me and my colleague and it became obvious to me that they knew each other. This was perfect timing for her to come by! And it got better too! She then provided me with another cash deposit and said that her friend Mary would be attending with her as well. It was exciting to have more people registering for my workshop. I thanked her and before I could ask her for her name and contact details, she dashed off again, assuming that I knew exactly who she was and who her friend Mary was. So, instead, I asked my colleague that just happened to be sitting with me in my office at such a convenient time. "Do you know her name?" I asked, and of course, he did. He was able to provide me with her full name and her email address, so I could register her and follow up with her appropriately. What a relief and such perfect timing! When I asked the Divine to help me find out more information about this woman, I never would have imagined that it also meant I would see an old colleague and have another person register for the workshop too! I could have forced the issue and wandered around the office trying to find her or someone who knew her name but when I let go and asked for help the

Divine was able to arrange the solution in a much more fun and fabulous way!

7) It is essential to remember that the Divine is all-knowing and able to organize things in infinite ways. And sometimes when we least expect things, is the exact moment that they can happen or manifest. As I was planning and organizing a weekend-long Yoga Retreat in Ontario, the spots were filling up quickly and I was very much looking forward to teaching yoga for a wonderful group of women. My neighbors, who were a mother and daughter, had signed up and paid to attend the retreat and were also looking forward to an enlightening weekend away. The mother called me one afternoon, disappointed, and explained that her daughter, unfortunately, was not able to get the weekend off work and so they would have to cancel. I stopped by to chat with her on my walk that evening as she only lived a few doors down. We talked about other potential retreats I would be hosting in the future and the reasons why her daughter was not able to get the weekend off work. After arranging to refund her money for the retreat, the mother said to me, "Just watch, my daughter will come home and tell me she has the weekend off work now" and we laughed about it. I had not really given it much of a second thought and went on my way for the rest of my walk that evening. I quietly said to the Divine while on my walk that if they are meant to join me for the retreat, that it be arranged in the most convenient and effortless way possible. Just two hours later I received a phone call from the mother saying... "You're never going to guess what happened! My daughter came home and said she now has the weekend off work so

we're going to come on the retreat. Didn't I say that was going to happen? Anyway, we're excited about the weekend now". Laughing we got off the phone and my heart simply filled with gratitude for the infinite arranging and rearranging power of the Divine. At that moment, I realized that there is nothing to ever really worry about and that sometimes things are just meant to be. I also decided that my ability to rest my concerns or worries in the arms of the Divine was a skill that I wanted to continue to develop as it was making my life flow with grace and ease.

8) Synchronistic events also tend to happen when we hold an image in our mind and then let go of how that might unfold for us, without any expectations. While visiting the Kripalu Center for Yoga and Health in the Berkshires of Massachusetts, I decided in my mind that I would like to enjoy one of my meals there with the Facilitator of the Workshop that I was attending as he was very well known for his incredible work in the field of trauma and yoga. In my mind, I thought about all the questions I would ask him and the type of conversation we would have, should the situation unfold that I had some quality time with him. I also decided in my mind that I would like to spend some quality time with one of the Yoga Dance instructors there at Kripalu, as he was also very knowledgeable in the area of body movement and healing trauma. While in a relaxed state of flow for most of my time at the retreat, I simply trusted and knew that if it was meant to be, it would happen. At lunch, on my third day, I went outside to sit at one of the picnic tables and sat down at an empty table. Just two minutes later I heard someone ask me, "Do you mind

if I join you?" and it was the Kripalu Yoga Dance instructor that I had been looking forward to speaking with. Of course, I invited him to sit down and an effortless conversation ensued about how yoga and dance can help people heal from previous trauma since traumatic events are often held in the body. And just a few minutes later I again hear another voice over my shoulder, "Do you mind if I join you both?" and it was the Facilitator from the Trauma and Yoga Workshop that I was taking. Apparently, unbeknownst to me, they knew each other quite well from both working in the field! At this point, I just sat laughing inside. I knew that I wanted to have quality time with both fellow professionals during my stay at the retreat and now I was sitting having lunch with both of them at the same time! Seriously, I could not have planned or arranged something better than this. Or even dreamed of something better than this since the timing was so impeccable. For the next hour, I was able to have a wonderful conversation with these two other professionals and ask every burning question I had about yoga, trauma, dance and the process of healing. The connections and knowledge I gained that afternoon were priceless and I was incredibly grateful for the way they both freely shared their expertise and experience. Even more so, I was grateful for the Divine arranging such a synchronistic event!

9) This next experience was a few synchronistic events that happened in a row which seems to happen as one develops the trust in the Divine and the ability to stay in flow for longer durations. This event also reminded me that the Divine is all-knowing and especially aware of all your favorite things! I had

gone to the local market on a Saturday to pick up fresh flowers for a friend's birthday. As I was wandering around and enjoying all that the local vendors had to offer, a random piece of paper flew off one of the tables just as I was walking by, almost stopping me in my tracks. I picked up the paper and handed it back to the vendor and she apologized and explained that she wasn't sure what just happened. I smiled and as I began to walk away I noticed on the vendor table just next to her was a variety of yummy items made from sweet potatoes which were my absolute favorite! I speak to the man about all the baking he does with sweet potatoes and decided to buy some muffins. He tells me that they're closing in about fifteen minutes, so he would like to give me all the muffins he has left for half price. I am laughing inside and beaming on the outside with gratitude. I accept the offer and thank him for his generosity. As I walk away, I'm wondering how the Divine knows that sweet potatoes are my favorite and how the Divine was able to arrange that piece of paper to fly off the table at just the right time so that I would stop there as I would have just walked right by if it hadn't stopped me.

Smiling, I wander over to the to exit doors of the market only to realize that it's absolutely pouring rain outside and I have no desire to get wet or sprint as fast as I can to my car. Unfortunately, I had left my umbrella in my car as it wasn't raining when I had originally gone into the market. As I stood by the exit doors watching the rain, I was thinking that I could either wait for the rain to let up before leaving or that maybe, just maybe, some kind person would walk me to their car with their umbrella. Less than one minute later, low and behold, the Divine arranged another synchronistic event for me. Two total strangers, a husband, and wife were on their way out of the market. They smiled at me and I smiled back. The woman asked me if I had an umbrella and I said I did not. She encouraged her husband to walk me to my car and he agreed without any hesitation. They just happened to have a large golf-sized umbrella so that neither of us would get wet. Of course, I again graciously accepted the offer and the lovely gentleman walked me to my car with their umbrella and then went back to pick up his wife from the market. I drove away, with free sweet potato muffins and not a drop of rain on me! The coincidences and the spectacular timing left me with a feeling of awe and deep connection to the Divine Universe.

10) To my amazement, the Divine is also able to rearrange multiple things at a time in order to ensure the best possible outcome. As someone who is a "planner", my challenge has been to recognize that the Divine can do a much more magnificent job of planning things but only if I let go, trust and follow, just like on the dance floor. So, after five months of attempting to sell an item that I had listed on an online classified website I had finally decided to give the item instead to a friend in Toronto who would be able to sell it for me because of his access to a different market. He lived about an hour away from me. We had arranged to meet at 2 pm on a Saturday afternoon so I could drop off the item and at approximately 11:30 am as I was preparing to leave the house, I had three emails come through at the same time on my smartphone. I decided to check them before leaving. The first email was a potential buyer from the online classified website,

offering me almost exactly what I had the item listed for. This was very exciting news, but it also meant that if I took the offer that it was not necessary for me to drive to Toronto at 2 pm. The second email that came through was from a girlfriend that I had not seen for months as she lives about three hours away. She explained that she just happened to be in the area today and wondered if I wanted to meet for coffee or late lunch. Well, that would be possible but only if I decided to take the new offer for my item and not drive to Toronto. The third email was from a lovely man I had been dating for some time and was clear about his intentions to move forward in the relationship although I was undecided. We had been discussing which direction the relationship would head for the past week or so and he was checking in with me while he was away. Within about ten minutes, my entire day changed because of these three synchronistic emails!

I decided to go with the flow and emailed back the new buyer from the online website and stated that I would accept the offer and asked how we should proceed. I called my friend in Toronto and explained that I would not be coming to Toronto at 2 pm to drop off the item because I had another potential buyer and my friend stated they were happy for me and wished me luck. Then I emailed my girlfriend back and agreed to meet at 1:30 pm for coffee. I also emailed back the man I was dating and explained that it might be best to talk when he got back from his trip away. As I sat down with my girlfriend for coffee just two hours later, we had the most interesting, entertaining conversation ever. She wanted to talk with me because the man she was dating at the time was letting her know about his intentions to move forward in the relationship and she wasn't sure how she felt and what to do. I laughed and explained that I was in the exact same situation with my relationship at the moment, so I wasn't sure how much help I could be. We just chatted about our options, what felt right and following our hearts. Then she explained to me that she was also trying to sell one of her personal items on an online classified website recently but was having difficulties and was now exploring other options. Again, I laughed and explained that I had waited for five months to try to sell something online, but it wasn't until I had given up on the idea and decided to move on to a different method that a legitimate offer came through, which just happened to be today. We agreed that there was obviously some form of Divine intervention earlier that rearranged my day to ensure that she and I could meet and share our stories. The following day I met with the buyer from the online classified site and successfully sold the item. We both felt content and satisfied with the transaction and left feeling blessed to have met each other, although brief, the transaction was significant and perfect timing. Again, I was left in amazement with the ability of the Divine to arrange and rearrange so many events at one time. And I thought I was a good planner! Ha! Apparently, letting go and letting the Divine take over was a much better option in this case.

11) This next synchronistic event was one that reminded me that it is important to be aware of where we place our attention and focus because what we focus on continues to grow and expand in our lives. In this instance, the Divine timing of things falling into place was magnificent. A friend of mine who

was a professional Ballroom and Latin Dance instructor had expressed interest in planning and hosting a retreat together that combined Salsa Dancing and Yoga. We had discussed this fun and exciting idea briefly at a dance social event one evening, and about a month later he emailed me asking for details about the Yoga Retreat in Costa Rica that I had hosted many retreats at before, thinking that it would one of the best places for us to host our combined retreat. It was a busy morning for me, so I decided I would email him later with details. As I went into work at the office later that day, I started chatting with a colleague about the CEO of the agency who was away on holidays at the moment. My colleague explained our CEO had gone to Costa Rica for two weeks. He then asked me about where I used to host Yoga Retreats in Costa Rica and the name and location of the place. I explained to him that it was called Pura Vida Spa and that it was located just twenty minutes outside the San Jose airport, one of my favorite places in the world. I explained to my colleague that my friend and I were considering hosting a Salsa Dance and Yoga Retreat together sometime soon.

A few hours later, I checked my email as I normally would, only to find an email from the Pura Vida Spa Yoga Retreat in Costa Rica. Seriously, I couldn't believe it at first and then I remembered that these things happen for me all the time. The email was not a general newsletter from the Retreat but rather a specific email to me directly, asking me if I was considering hosting another yoga retreat anytime soon since my retreats in the past had been so successful. The email also had a list of three weeks that were still available for February 2015 to bring down a group of students and host a retreat. After thanking the Divine for such amazing timing for the email, I forwarded the information on to my friend who wanted to host the Salsa Dancing Yoga Retreat with me and explained what a fascinating day I had. Does synchronistic timing get any better? I'm not sure but I'm also not complaining either because at that moment I was particularly impressed with the Divine's ability to organize my day in such a way.

12) I'm often overwhelmed with excitement and gratitude even with the smallest synchronistic event. Sometimes though, the arranging of a parking spot, for example, can be so much more than just that. It's more about the perfect timing and simply allowing life to flow in an easy and effortless way. This experience started with having a blissful, magical day at a Yoga Conference in Toronto. After practicing about six hours of yoga that day I was in a beautiful state of flow and felt connected to the Divine. I arrived at my girlfriend's condo complex after the conference. We had planned to stay in, have dinner and return to the conference the next morning. Parking at her condo complex sometimes posed a bit of a challenge as there was limited visitor parking and the remaining parking spots were specifically marked for tenants. Today was one of those days where there was no visitor parking available. I quietly asked the Divine to help me find a parking spot as I drove around the lot for the third time. I called my friend to ask for any suggestions as I wasn't having any luck finding a spot. Seemingly unsuccessful, I acquiesce and park on the side street instead. I head up to her condo, explain where I've parked and proceed to enjoy dinner and delightful

conversation. A few hours later she suggests that I head back down to check if there are any visitor parking spots now available. I debate with her and explain that I'm sure it's fine to park on the side street overnight. She reminds me that I have received a parking ticket once before in the area because of where I parked and although I have parked in a different area this time, she did not want me to get another ticket. She suggests that I go down to check for visitor parking and that if I see anyone in the process to ask them about parking on the side street. And I think to myself, "Really? What are the odds of me seeing a random stranger who knows the rules of the roads here?" I surrender to her suggestion, albeit with a little resistance, put my coat and shoes on and head downstairs.

As I exit from the front door of her condo building, I start to turn left to head towards my car that's parked on the side street but out of the corner of my eye, I catch a glimpse of a man walking towards the front door. A little nudge from the Divine says "Ask him. Go on. Ask him." And so, I do. I turn around and ask the man if he knows if I can park on the side street overnight. He explains to me that unfortunately that is not permitted and that I would receive a ticket if I left it there overnight. He asks if I'm staying with someone in the building and I explain that my girlfriend lives there, and I just need a visitor parking spot for the night but that they're all full. He asks what time I plan on leaving in the morning and I tell him that I will be gone by 10 am. He then says, "Well, I just moved my car into this handicapped parking spot here because I have a special sticker. However, I also own parking spot #42 which is right there". He points literally 10 feet away from us to an empty parking spot. I turn my head slightly to peak around his car and see just how close the spot really is. He politely says, "You can park there for the night if you like. I don't mind at all." I start beaming and radiating with excitement. "Really...are you sure?" I ask. He reinforces that he doesn't want to see me get a ticket and that he is happy to share his parking spot for the night. I genuinely thank him with a huge smile on my face although I was quite sure he could feel my gratitude radiating out from every fiber of my being. I skip down the sidewalk to my car, so happy that I forget to even ask the man his name. I move my car and settle it into spot #42 for the night. After heading back up to my girlfriend's condo and telling her of the absolute amazing timing of running into that man, I thank her for telling me to ask a stranger about parking if I saw one. On my way out in the morning, I placed a thank you card on the windshield of the man's car which was still in the handicapped spot. At that point, I was simply feeling gratitude, gratitude and more gratitude. Sometimes it's just a parking spot but sometimes it seems like so much more than that. Every part of me knows that when I ask the Divine for help, even with the little things, that solutions are guaranteed to be provided and those solutions are always in ways that I could not have possibly thought of or arranged myself. It just feels like magic...there are no other words to describe it.

13) There are many times when a synchronistic event occurs that I find myself simply in a state of awe because there is no way that I could have arranged something better! There was a day when a colleague came into my office to discuss his

experience of becoming a first-time home buyer. He explained that he needed a local real estate agent that could perhaps help him with the process as he had a lot of questions as a first-time home buyer. He also mentioned that he may ask another colleague at the office for some help as she was also a realtor for a company called Coldwell Banker. I let him know that if I thought of anyone that could be of help, I would let him know. Later that same day I was at home in my living room talking on the phone when I looked out the window and it seemed as though this random man was simply birthed out of the quantum field and was now walking up my sidewalk. In his hand, he was holding a stack of notepads. It looked like the type of notepad that you would stick up on your fridge to write your grocery list perhaps. He rang my doorbell, I told my dad that I was on the phone with to hang on, and then answered the door. When I did, the man asked me if I was thinking of buying or selling my home. I replied that I wasn't sure and asked why. He offered me one of the notepads and said, "We've got a great deal for first time home buyers if you or anyone you know is considering doing so." I smiled and laughed and took the pad of paper and said thank you. Once I had shut the front door, I looked at the pad of paper, and laughed even more! At the top of the pad of paper was a logo for Coldwell Banker, the picture of a realtor and his contact info. Below that was a hand-written note by this realtor stating that he was offering an exceptional deal for first time home buyers and a low-down payment and to contact him for further information. Obviously, the Divine had been listening to the conversation I had earlier that day with my colleague! I brought the piece of paper to the office the next day and handed the paper to my colleague letting him know that I was pretty sure this information was meant for him and not me.

14) And let's not forget that whatever we place our attention on is where our energy will be flowing. And that sometimes we are unaware even that we are asking for the Divine to assist us, even with the little things. I was on the phone one day with my Mom's new dentist, planning for her first appointment and providing all her basic details. When the receptionist at the dental office asked me for my mom's postal code, I realized that I did not know it off the top of my head and so told her that I would have to get back to her with her postal code later. She explained that would be fine and to contact her when I could. Later that same day, I happened to be out shopping for groceries with my mom and when we got to the check out the strangest coincidence happened! As she was packing my mom's groceries, she asked my mom if she could have her postal code! The clerk explained they were doing some market research to find out where their customers were coming from and so my mom was happy to provide the clerk with her postal code which of course, I overheard, and simply smiled inside, making note of it so I could call the dental office back and let them know. Then I silently thanked the Divine for reminding me that I was asking about that earlier. And another reminder that the Divine is always with us, listening to every thought we think and every word we say.

15) Sometimes when we are consciously connecting with the Divine daily, things that we ask for or need can simply fall into

place in the most effortless way. Like the quote from the Bible (Matthew 7:7) "Ask, and it shall be given to you; seek, and ye shall find; knock, and it shall be opened unto you". On New Year's Day of 2010, I wrote down on a piece of paper that it was my intention to create an Emotional Freedom Technique (E.F.T.) product of some type in 2010, so that I could teach and help more people. I had no idea how that would happen, and nor did I spend any time worrying about how or when that process might unfold. Unexpectedly and randomly, about three months later, I received an email from an online marketing professional who asked me if I would be interested in creating educational videos teaching E.F.T. as well as writing a book about technique. Just like that! Of course, we negotiated, and I agreed to produce the videos and write the book. It required taking action, however, the process was smooth and effortless, with the support of the Divine bringing the online marketer and myself together. Similarly, another amazing synchronicity occurred when looking for a publisher for my second book. I had spent a few days meditating what it would feel like emotionally to connect with a publisher, allowing the excitement to radiate within my energy field. About a week later I attended a Kundalini yoga class and noticed a new woman in class that had just started attending the past few weeks. After yoga class, everyone stayed for tea and a friend of mine just happened to know the new woman and she politely introduced us. At the same time, my friend suggests that this woman tell me about her new book! This woman and I proceed to chat about her book and my book and she explained that she just signed with a publisher in

British Columbia and without any hesitation, offers to recommend me and introduce me to her publisher. What perfect timing and a natural connection! Keep in mind that it's not that you don't need to take action when a synchronistic event does happen, and things seem to just fall into place for you. It's just that the journey to get there is one of ease and flowing instead of forcing. Experiencing synchronistic events in your life is one way of knowing that you're in a state of allowing and connecting with the Divine.

16) On very a challenging day, where life seemed to be falling apart at the edges, I turned to the Divine for assistance, truly knowing how powerful the Divine can be at rearranging things. At the end of this challenging day, I was walking outside my condo to get something out of my car and I looked up to the sky and said, "Alright Divine, I need a miracle for this one! There is nothing else I can do for this situation and I need your help. Amaze me with a miracle, please and thank you!" I got what I needed from my car, returned to my condo, put on my comfy pajamas and settled in for the evening. About two hours later, there was an unexpected knock at my front door. I thought quickly who it might be but knew that I had not invited anyone over. I went to answer the door and found a familiar face! It was a friend and student from one of my yoga classes. I opened the door and she apologized for dropping by unannounced but found a book that she wanted me to have as she thought it would be perfect for me. It just happened to be "Spirit Junkie: A Radical Road to Self-Love and Miracles" by Gabrielle Bernstein. I was familiar with the book as it has teachings in it from A Course in Miracles. I laughed joyously

and thanked my friend for dropping off the book with impeccable timing that she was unaware of. As I sat down on my couch with the book I thought, "Wow Divine, you are FAST! That was impressive." Of course, as I dived into the book it had all the lessons and teachings that I required to get through the challenging time I was experiencing. Priceless, really.

17) During this process of connecting with the Divine and manifesting what you're focused on it's also important to note that the Divine only knows abundance so be careful what you wish for! I was working one evening on my website, updating information on my "Enlightened Yoga Parties" page, refining the details of my service to host yoga classes or events for others in their home or venue. Mostly local women were drawn to the opportunity to have an Enlightened Yoga Party for a special occasion. When I was done with the webpage updates I decided to shower before bed. While in the shower I started thinking that I needed to head to the drug store the next day. I was leaving for a trip to Mexico in a few weeks and wanted to pick up some travel size shampoo and conditioner as I knew they would be easier to pack. These two points of focus, the yoga parties, and the shampoo and conditioner seemed unrelated in my mind until the next morning when my cell phone rang. It was a random phone number calling from British Columbia that I normally wouldn't even answer but there was a little nudge from the Divine that said, "go ahead, answer it" and so I did. The woman introduced herself as a representative from Pantene Pro V Hair products and asked if I was still hosting Enlightened Yoga Parties. Intrigued by

where this might be going, I told her that yes, in fact, I was on occasion. She explained that they had a new product line they were launching and were looking to give away travel size shampoo and conditioner to business owners like myself who could share them with yoga students and fitness clients. They were attempting to market to women who practiced yoga and exercised. She asked if she could send me some samples of their new shampoo and conditioner and I agreed. We finished up the conversation as I provided her with my mailing address and she said that she was going to send me 300 travel size shampoo and conditioner bottles!! I laughed and agreed that would be fine. Just in time for my travels to Mexico, a box arrived on my doorstep containing 300 bottles of shampoo and conditioner. I graciously thanked the Divine for the overwhelming abundance and said next time I would be more specific if I only needed one of something! The Divine, again, is also known to have a sense of humor at times.

18) Sometimes for even random thoughts and conversations, we are having the Divine is listening to and finding a way to let us know that it is listening. On a cold November morning, I texted my boyfriend asking him to remind me to pick up Vitamin B6 later that day because I was running low. I laughed as I texted him that one way to remember was to think of that song we heard at the gym on the weekend called, "Like a V6" and he texted me back and said he thought the song was called "Like a G6"?! He explained that a "G6" is one of the fastest airplanes. I replied and said I must have been thinking of a V6 engine in a car. We finished messaging back and forth and I went about my morning. About 3 hours later I was driving

home only to find that the road was blocked about two blocks from my driveway. There was a yellow "Road Closed" caution sign and some city workers that seemed quite busy. I decided that I would just drive around the block and enter my driveway from the other side. Since I had never taken the back-side streets around I was just hoping I would find my way. I turned right on the nearest side street and found myself behind another red car now. I wondered if they knew their way around the neighborhood and perhaps, I could follow them to get around this roadblock detour. I took a moment to ask myself how I had attracted this experience into my life. I believe all experiences, good or bad, either have a lesson for us or are brought to us by the Divine for some reason. Still unsure of the answer, I continued to follow this red car around the back-side streets and then turned back onto the main road and sat waiting behind the car at a stop light. A little voice inside told me to look closer at the car that was guiding me. I laughed and laughed! The car I was following was a Pontiac G6 with a V6 engine in it!! Right on the back of the car, there was a Pontiac logo with a G6 logo and a V6 logo as well. As the light turned green, I continued to follow the car that just happened to go left again, around the block, guiding me right back home. I thought to myself that my question had obviously been answered! The lesson was that the Divine is always listening to us and can guide us home. Initially, what seemed to be a frustrating experience of a roadblock turned out to be a beautiful blessing in disguise!

19) It is always important to be clear with the Divine about what you are asking for, either with your meditation or your

vibration. And the Divine will clearly mirror back to you what you are asking for or what you are focusing on. I often practiced meditation where I would clearly imagine what I wanted to draw into my life and then feel gratitude for the Divine as if my prayers had already been answered. In this specific meditation, I chose to focus on two different things. The first thing was feeling gratitude for having another person sign up and confirm their attendance at my sixth Costa Rica Yoga retreat that I was planning and hosting. It was my intention to bring as many people as I could for this fabulous experience and thanked the Divine for sending me more students that were ready to attend. I took a moment to release that intention before moving on to my second intention. The second thing was feeling gratitude for being a published author and speaker, traveling on the speaking circuit. I had already published my first book and was in the process of looking for a publisher for my second book. I was also being offered more speaking opportunities at the time. Again, in my meditation, I felt as though my prayers had already been answered and I was experiencing a whole other level of great success as a published author and speaker. Now, the very next morning after this meditation, I woke to find a wonderful surprise. I had received an email from someone that I had never met before that was excited and ready to book the Costa Rica Yoga Retreat and wanted to move forward with payment. The feeling of joy and gratitude I felt was the same as in my meditation the evening prior. And the most entertaining part was that when I read to the bottom of the email it was signed by a lovely woman named Grace Cirocco and under her name, it stated, "Published

Author and Speaker" and had her website as well. Of course, I smiled to myself. I was looking for another retreat participant but didn't think it was her who would be the author and speaker! Although, my two intentions were separate in my mind and my meditation, the Divine did a miraculous job of blending the two together! Lesson learned about how to be specific with what you ask for because the Divine can work in mysterious ways.

20) The other lesson I have learned from countless synchronistic events is to be mindful of my everyday thoughts and let the Divine know exactly what I'm looking for. Sometimes even my mind wanders to negative thoughts but the most important part is simply noticing and redirecting. I was working out at a gym that was new to me in Buffalo, New York and found my mind wandering while doing cardio. There was "negative" news on the six big television screens in front of me and thought to myself that there were only negative people living in Buffalo and no one that I really felt I resonated with. Catching myself in that thought, I realized that was not necessarily true and that thinking that way certainly wasn't going to help me align with any positive people. I realized that if there were positive people in this gym or in Buffalo that I would have to tell my brain and the Divine to look for them, find them or meet them. So, I said silently in my mind to the Divine, "if there are any positive, high vibrating, yogis or spiritual people in this gym or in Buffalo please help me find them". I made a conscious choice to trust and let go and simply move on with my workout, not attached to how short or how long the process may take. When I finished doing

cardio I wandered over to the weights and started with the leg press machine. Before getting on the machine I did a modified downward facing dog to stretch a little and then got started. At this point, a man that I had never met before walked up to me and asked how my workout was going and if I practiced yoga. It was almost as if he appeared out of nowhere as I had never seen him there before. We got chatting about yoga and my teaching background and it turned out that he was the owner of the Rising Sun Yoga Studio that I had been going to in Buffalo for classes the past few months! We had a great conversation about getting connected to the yoga community in Buffalo and exchanged business contact information. We agreed to stay in touch and just like that I had shifted my entire perspective of the "negative" gym to see the positive that was already there. I could not have asked the Divine to connect me with a more positive, high vibration, spiritual yogi. The most important thing I realized that day was to be mindful of my thoughts and redirect as needed. After all, the Divine is always listening.

These are just a few of the examples from the original list of 200 events that I started with in my Synchronicity Journal. Although my life is now filled with so many synchronistic events that I don't even have the time to write them all down anymore what's most important about this list is for you to come to understand and believe that this way of living, in effortless flow, is a state that is available to each and every one of us, should we choose to focus our attention and remain open to the opportunity to experience life in this manner. The Divine loves us so much that it desires to see us happy and living a life that fulfills us in many ways and can create beautiful events of perfect timing for us at any given moment. However, because we have free will because we can make our own choices, the Divine can only help us if we let go of control and allow room for synchronistic events to happen. We can focus our attention and let the Divine know what type of feeling or emotion we would like to experience by simply shifting our mind's attention in that direction, however, we do not get to decide "how" it will "happen" or when. This is where the letting go part comes in!

To be more specific, here are some dance steps to practice in order to start living a life full of magical events and experience the manifesting of miracles:

Step One: Start and maintain a Synchronicity Journal (there is a matching one available with this book)

Step Two: Focus your attention on what you desire to create in your life.

Step Three: Feel the emotion and radiate the vibration of that desire as if it already exists in your life.

Step Four: Let go of any expectations or plans of how it will come into your life. Let the Divine lead you.

Again, let's elaborate on these steps.

Step One:

Start and maintain a Synchronicity Journal

At your next earliest convenience, go out and buy yourself a new journal specifically for writing down any and all events that feel like synchronicity, serendipity, coincidence, magic or miracles for you. There is a "Step into Synchronicity" Journal that has been designed as a companion to this book as well. Keep the journal somewhere that you can see it so that you will be constantly reminded that you're looking for these types of events to occur in your life daily. Why would you take the time and effort to do this? Simply because whatever we focus our attention on continues to grow and expand in our lives so the more we focus on living life connected to the Divine and loving synchronistic events every time they happen, the more we open the door for the Divine to provide other similar experiences. The idea is to get excited about starting this journal and looking forward to synchronistic events. At the same time, synchronistic events cannot be forced or brought on by our will. Getting your journal ready is more akin to letting the Divine know that you're open and ready for the experience. When you do have an event happen that has that synchronistic feeling to it, no matter how small or seemingly insignificant it is, write it down in your new journal! Take a moment to thank the Divine and feel a deeper sense of gratitude in your heart, for the wonderful experience that just happened. A sense of awe, wonder and excitement often occurs during synchronistic events as well so stay in that place of feeling and that vibration as long as you can. The Divine also has a wonderful sense of humor when it comes to aligning us with things that we've been asking for or focusing our attention on. By that I mean the synchronistic event will likely leave you with at least a smile on your face if not in a deep belly laugh because of the humor and creativity involved in the situation.

You are not limited to just writing these events down in a journal. Perhaps you want to tell others about it or write it in an email to someone you know or write a blog post about it. The point is that the more often you repeat the story by telling it to others or writing it down and feeling the magical feeling of the whole experience, the more you radiate and vibrate at that level, which is like sending a signal to the Divine that you would like to experience these things more often. If you have ever had a synchronistic event happen at any point in your life, I would encourage you to start your journal by writing those down. Maybe they were small, or maybe there were very significant. Regardless, opening the journal and writing down wonderful little miracles that you've experienced before on that fresh, first page is the perfect way to start your new habit and way of life. It also indicates to the Divine that you're ready for more! And if you've never had what you believe to be a synchronistic event happen in your life than simply write on the first page a title that indicates that this journal is reserved for all events that feel like synchronicity, serendipity, coincidence, magic or miracles. Then simply watch and wait patiently for them to be drawn into your life.

Step Two:
Focus your attention on what you desire to create in your life.

The synchronicities that will occur in your life will inevitably be related to what you've been thinking about or what you've been placing your attention on. We have approximately 60000 thoughts a day and 80-90% of those thoughts are the same as the day before. So, if you desire to create something new or different in your life then that means you must begin to think differently. Take some time to write down, perhaps in your synchronicity journal, what you desire to create in your life. Perhaps you desire to create a new career or a new relationship or an opportunity to travel or an improved level of health. Whatever it is that you'd like to create in your life it's important to be specific. List the specific expectations of the new job or the specific qualities of the new person you will be meeting. List exactly where you would like to travel to and what sort of activities you would engage in if you were as healthy as you'd like to be.

The most important part is then to focus your attention on this desire each day. What may happen is that you will be distracted by your current reality in which this specific desire does not currently exist. This can lead only to synchronicities that are related to your current reality. This is welcome, of course, if you currently love your reality and wouldn't change a thing. If you're looking to connect with the Divine for guidance to experience synchronicities and live a different life than it's important to make the Divine aware of exactly what you desire in your life. Synchronistic events are typically in line with your current level of thinking because the Divine is all-knowing and is aware of every thought you have. Yes, every thought you have. And so, the synchronistic event must be at the same level of your current vibration which is a direct reflection of your thoughts. Hence the importance of focusing your mind's attention on what you do desire to have in your life.

Step Three:
Feel the emotion and radiate the vibration of that desire as if it already exists in your life.

Sounds easy enough doesn't it? Most of us speak about what we desire to have in our lives but do so from a place of lack. Sometimes just the act of being conscious of what experiences we would like to have in our life makes us become acutely aware that they are not currently a part of our reality. This acknowledgment is the first step. Recognizing what we don't currently have in our life simply allows us to become aware of what we do want in our lives. The next step is to close your eyes, withdraw from your current reality, and imagine what it would feel like to have this desired event or experience in your life. I mean feel it with all your heart. The emotion needs to be radiating in every cell of your body and out of every pore in your skin so that it can vibrate within your surroundings. Hold this thought, emotion, and vibration for as long as you can. If this event or experience that you desire already existed in your life you would also feel deeply grateful for it. Feel the emotion of gratitude so much that you convince yourself that it's already part of your life. True, deep-felt gratitude that comes from your heart should have the ability to move you to tears. Literally, having tears streaming down your face because the emotion you feel is so real. Only that level of belief and emotion can shift and change the vibration that surrounds you and simultaneously signals to the Divine that you are ready and worthy of drawing this experience into your life – but only because you radiate like it already does. Feel the feeling of that which you desire before it arrives in your life....and watch how the Divine finds a way to create the coincidence of events in perfect timing to bring who and what you need into your life, exactly when you need it!

Step Four:
Let go of any expectations of how or when it will come into your life. Let the Divine lead you.

This part is the most paradoxical. It's the easiest because the Divine takes over for you to create events and circumstances beyond your wildest dreams and yet it is also the most difficult because it can be very challenging to "let go" and not worry about when or how something will show up in our lives. Especially when it's something you deeply desire or that you may have struggled to create in your life for a long period of time. The feeling of letting go and allowing the Divine to create your desired outcome has the potential to be one of the most trusting and beautiful experiences you can have. Once you develop that level of trust with the Divine you will never worry again a day in your life. The experience of letting go can be difficult to describe, but it's analogous to being on a swing set. Imagine for a moment that you're back at a playground that you once frequented as a child. You're on your favorite swing set, with the breeze blowing through your hair and the sounds of fellow friends playing in the near distance. Imagine swinging so high that there's that moment of absolute, total freedom at the top where you're completely suspended in the air, just for a split second. You get that rush through your body as you're launched for a moment into total bliss and weightlessness, and not being able to resist laughter pouring out from deep in your belly. And even though you're flying through the air you're not afraid one bit. You're excited and exhilarated but there's not an ounce of fear because you know that the swing is there to catch you. With total faith and trust, you continue to swing higher and higher because you know you're safe and supported. There is never a moment of doubt that the swing will catch you on the way back down from the peak height but only a sense of liberation and reliance on the support of the swing set to catch you. This is what it feels like to truly trust and let go, allowing the Divine to lead you and support you on the way to what you desire.

If you try to force or create the event yourself, you may be successful. However, in this instance, the "solution" can only come from the same level of mind that likely created your current situation to begin with. We must think, feel and vibrate at a different level in order to allow the Divine to lead us to a different solution. This means that as we truly let go that we are no longer responsible for "how" or "when" the event occurs in our life. Just like when we are dancing with a partner on the dance floor. One person leads, and one person follows. The leader knows "how" to indicate the next move to their partner and exactly "when" to provide the next move in order to stay connected to the music and continue to flow together. It is the responsibility of the one who is "following" to stay neutral and not anticipate. If they anticipate the next move because they think they know what would be best, the partnership falls apart because resistance will begin occurring between the two people. Therefore, it is important to stay neutral and be prepared to go in any direction or turn in any way, at any given time, with only a moment's notice. There is no getting to decide how or when a turn will occur and as scary as it can be to totally let go of control and simply remain in a neutral state, the wonder and experience of being in a state of magical flow that can happen when we do let go is absolutely priceless. Developing this level of trust can take time and practice like anything else. However, when we remind ourselves that this feeling can be like being on a swing or being guided in a waltz around a ballroom floor, it seems a little less scary and a little more intriguing.

You will know when you're experiencing a synchronistic event and that the Divine Universe is collaborating with you to co-create your desires, because of the distinct feeling that happens. It will feel as though, the person or situation, as it unfolds at that moment, is literally being "birthed" out of nothingness or being delivered from the field of infinite possibilities. Others describe it as similar to the unique feeling of déjà vu or a "glitch in the Matrix" if you've ever seen the movie. Once you have the experience of letting go and a magical, unexpected, synchronistic event happens for you and then you write it down in your journal because you're so fascinated by the experience, it is more likely to happen for you again. And over and over again!

Now, if you really want to know what's going on behind the scenes of the Divine Universe and how all this magic is really unfolding, make sure you've got your dance shoes on because we're about to learn a whole new dance step...

CHAPTER 4:

ADVANCED STEPS – DANCING IN THE WEB OF THE INTERCONNECTED UNIVERSE

We are all connected to the Divine and once we begin working in harmony with the Divine, we can truly co-create the most beautiful life. Having experiences that confirm that the Divine truly exists within each one of us can also strengthen our belief system and faith in the Divine. One of the best ways to connect and co-create with the Divine is to access the field of infinite vibration and begin to apply the theory of Quantum Law. Theoretically speaking, Quantum Law explains that we can consciously create our reality from the inside out. According to the law, the world we live in consists of "waves of infinite possibility" that happen to turn into "particles of experience" once we place our attention in the external world. These waves of possibility are simply responding to our vibration and belief system. The vibration that surrounds us is really an accumulation of our past thoughts, actions, experiences and patterns that we repeat. It is this vibration that creates the reality that we see each morning when we open our eyes. The world is a mirror for our current level of vibration. The good news is that the beginning of each day is also an opportunity to create a new reality by thinking a new thought, feeling a new emotion or having a new experience and changing a pattern. This is what allows us to create a new vibrational pattern and therefore create a new and different tomorrow.

Everything is vibration at the most subtle level. Initially, we begin by understanding this at an intellectual level and, eventually, through the practice of meditation, become proficient at feeling and sensing energy or vibration. And then finally, with more practice, we can become a master at shaping it. Perhaps you have read about Quantum Law and studied vibrational energy or attended lectures explaining the science behind this. This is the first step. The next step is to practice becoming fully aware of the present moment, quieting the mind and sensing the body in space in order to start to feel or sense or experience all things at this level of vibration. As you practice more and more, the art becomes more specific as you move into a state of meditation and connection with the infinite field and come into alignment with the Divine. From this place comes true co-creation as your intention and the intention of the Divine to express through you become a perfect match.

Teaching from a place of experience is something that is genuinely important to me and so I share from a place of having both the intellectual knowledge and being blessed with some extraordinary experiences that affirm my belief in the Divine every day. With the sharing of my experiences, my hope is that it strengthens your belief and connection with the Divine. I have been blessed with a few deeply profound experiences in my life where I had the opportunity to enter various altered states of consciousness and literally experience everything as vibration and to feel intricately connected to the Divine.

The first experience was in December of 2008 when I was visiting my favorite Yoga Retreat Centre, Pura Vida Spa in Costa Rica and decided to treat myself to a massage. The Wellness Centre there employs a variety of talented and gifted therapists including a blind massage therapist by the name of Olman. Due to his inability to see he has developed the gift of being extremely sensitive to touch and energy as well as being very intuitive. During the massage I could effortlessly release physical and emotional tension in my body, leaving me with a deeply relaxed sensation at the end. His hands had a healing property to them that was unlike any massage therapist I had been to before. That very night I had a miraculous dream. In the dream, Olman comes to me and explains to me everything in the entire Universe resonates as the vibration of "OM" (or AUM). He explains briefly that the sound of OM is what connects all things together, because everything, at the deepest level, is vibrating at this level. And for a few moments, I enter and experience this vibration. Words cannot describe how blissful and beautiful this experience truly was. For just a few moments in the dream, I dissolved into nothing more than the vibration of OM, the vibration of all that is. I awake from the dream with a sense of expansion and understanding.

The next experience comes sometime later in April of 2011 when I had another fascinating dream. The dream begins with me sitting on a purple yoga mat with another woman whom I immediately feel is a wise and profound teacher, however, I don't recognize her. She tells me that when you study the teachings of Buddha you will come to realize that you ARE God, that God is in everything, everyone and all around you. She explains to me that you create everything in your reality and that you are in fact, the Creator. The lesson is simple and straight forward. I wake up again from this dream with an overall sense of peace and knowing that I am a powerful Creator.

After that, I had an experience that was one of connecting to spirit while in a waking state as opposed to a dream. In January of 2014, I was lying in bed at night, trying to sleep, but being kept awake by my racing thoughts and anxious feelings. Being human and all, this worry would keep me up from time to time. As I was laying there, eyes closed, thoughts wandering, I suddenly felt a cold breeze on my right side. Not because the window was open or because there was a draft in the room, but because there was a Spirit or Angel beside me. There is a sense that this Spirit or Angel only has positive and loving intentions for me, so I consciously acknowledge its presence and indicate in my mind that I am open to whatever message they want to provide me with or help they want to provide me. It only takes a moment before I feel this Spirit move closer to me and it feels as though this Spirit literally embraces me with the most wonderful hug of Divine and supportive love possible. Think of a mother holding a newborn child with the most kind, gentle, nurturing intention…that's what it feels like. I simply surrender into this embrace and unconditional love and as I do, all the racing thoughts and feelings of anxiousness that I had just minutes before, simply melt away and transform into tears of gratitude that are now rolling down my cheeks. I also hear a message that specifically lets me know that everything will be alright, that there is no need to worry and that it's okay to relax. This message and a warm embrace from Spirit relaxes me into a state of deep sleep in an effortless way. The next morning, I awake from the most restful night of sleep that I've had in a very long time, feeling totally refreshed, connected to the Divine, in complete awe by the experience and deeply grateful for the support provided for me.

As I remained open to further experiences, they continued to happen for me.

The next experience occurred in February of 2014 when I went to bed at night, and as I was about to fall asleep, I felt the sensation of a cool breeze at my side which I knew was a Spirit Guide coming to visit me. I heard the male voice of this Spirit say "Hello?" and I responded by saying he could stay and visit if his intentions were loving and positive. Then I was shown a draw bridge that split open in the middle and I was invited to jump over from one side to the other. I agree to the invitation by taking a running start and leaping over the open middle to the other side of the bridge. Once I was there everything changed, and I felt a complete expansion of awareness because infinite possibilities exist on this side. There is some fear that I feel but I am comforted by the spirit guide that is with me. There was a feeling of having no physical body, no sense of time and no concept of space. I sense and experience that I am floating literally within an interconnected web of pure vibration that is delicately connected in so many ways. Almost like a spider web of interconnectedness that expands infinitely. He, the guide that is with me, is explaining to me how important it is to understand the interconnectedness of all things, that we are not separate from anyone or anything in our lives. I am also shown (because no actual words are spoken on this side) that this web is flexible, mutable and constantly fluctuating and responding to us and our intentions. I come to understand that this changeable web can be affected by one movement, one thought or a simple intention that we have. Just like spiders are known to be sensitive to vibratory stimulation on their webs, this web of interconnectedness is very sensitive and responds to our intentions. I come to know and understand that we, in fact, can shape and influence this web. I then feel that this is all I can absorb at this time and soon return to my physical body, lying safely in my bed. I feel incredibly groggy and a little confused as to how I have returned. I am acutely aware of the density of my physical body as I begin to move and stretch. The entire experience was as though I had been offered and taken the "red pill" to be shown the illusion of the "Matrix" and to come to understand the truth of our reality. The best way to summarize the experience is best said by the naturalist **John Muir...**

> *"Tug on anything at all and you'll find it connected to everything else in the universe."*

And just when I thought that the Divine Spirit was done teaching me lessons on how the Universe works, I was presented with another opportunity for learning.

This time it's April 2014 and again, I'm lying in bed at night, in that relaxed state, just prior to sleep. I receive the familiar feeling that Spirit is again with me and so I open my mind to whatever experience is about to occur. Spirit begins by showing me a simple marble. Initially, it looks like a regular marble that kids would play with and as I look closer and focus on the marble in my mind it begins to expand, and I come to understand that inside this marble contains the entire Universe of infinite possibilities. It is also explained to me that each of us is living in our consciously created reality, which is contained within this marble. Almost like we all live in our own little vibrational bubble that appears solid and real but is more malleable and pliable than we think. Then in a moment, I slip into the marble and now find myself within the marble instead of looking at it from the outside. Within the marble are infinite possibilities though and it feels like I have been brought there to learn. It feels as though I am now training for the practical application of Quantum Law. It feels like Harry Potter Wizard School for lack of a better descriptive term. In order to expand on the theory of Quantum Law, I'm being encouraged and shown how to put it into practice. I then find myself sitting at an office chair in a group counseling room at my current place of work. Although the room is normally filled with many people when I'm facilitating a group, this time the room is empty and there is no pressure.

I was holding onto a metal Tibetan singing bowl in my left hand and played the bowl just for a few moments. It is then explained to me that in this "classroom", everything is supple, changeable vibration and not as solid as it seems. I am invited to exercise this belief and use my intention to command matter to change. And so, I do. I turned my gaze to the metal singing bowl and I simply decided that I would like to melt the metal. I used my intention to command the metal to begin to melt and so it does and as it melts around my hand, I then decide to turn it into a metal glove and it responds to my intention. There is a delicate balance of commanding and willing it to transform into a glove as opposed to "trying" to melt it into that state. There is a firm belief that I have the ability to mold and shape this melted metal into whatever I desire. This glove is a perfect fit for my hand and I turn my hand to look at how it has shaped around both the front and the back of my hand. Now what? Well, I decided to continue the experiment by turning the metal glove back into the singing bowl. With the same intention and will, the same balance between knowing I have the power and not forcing, the metal begins to transform from the glove back into the singing bowl. It is as though the metal simply responds to my thought and my intention. The metal is still soft and supple and so the transformation happens easily, and I find the bowl back in the palm of my left hand identical to the original shape and size. Like magic! It is again, explained to me that each one of us can do this in our lives should we seek to practice and develop this power and collaborate with the Divine. I then find myself moving back outside of the marble and become aware of my physical body, lying in bed again, coming back to my current reality.

The process continues about a week later as I have a very similar experience. Now I start to feel like I'm enrolled in the School of Infinite Awareness and there's no turning back! As I climb into bed and close my eyes, I'm acutely aware that I'm awake still but start to feel the cold breeze which is the presence of Spirit again. Silently, I let Spirit know that I sense its presence and I'm open to the teachings or lessons it has for me. I feel Spirit merge with my physical body and take a very deep full breath in. As I exhale my body relaxes deeply in an effortless way. It feels as though my body begins to dissipate into pure vibration and expand out in all directions. It's as though "I" disappear and become merged with the Quantum field of infinite possibilities. This time the experience is so intense that fear arises in me and I pull back a bit, letting Spirit know that I'm not ready yet and that I would just like to practice moving back into my body and then returning to the state of infinity. As so, with my intention, I simply move back to sensing and feeling my physical body and then relax and let go again in the Quantum field. After practicing a few times, I begin to feel more confident and ready for the next step and so I let Spirit know I'm ready again. Then there is an empty space in front of me and it is explained to me that I can create something or anything out of this space by using my intention and my mind. At first, I'm at a loss of where to start as there are literally infinite options. In this realm, it is just as easy to create a skyscraper as it is a paperclip. There are no limitations, only limitations set by my own mind. And so, I begin by creating a bright red door with a silver handle. As I open the door to walk through it, on the other side is a blissful beach paradise where the weather is perfect, and the sand is soft. After spending some time creating palm trees and sitting on a beach blanket I decide to walk back through the red door. I then begin to create various experiences just for the purpose of exploring and to practice shapeshifting. Within this infinite field, I create a glass of water and turn it into a glass of red wine with my intention and focus. The water slowly starts turning red and becomes darker and darker until it's pure wine. And for practice, I then turn it back into the glass of water, simply reversing the process.

I then ask the Divine to show me the next level or lesson and I am invited to practice transforming energy and fears. As fear begins to arise, I am reminded of the importance to connect with the Divine and so I use my intention to feel strongly connected with the power of Divine energy and begin to radiate a white light all around me and in my surroundings. The sense of fear simply dissolves all on its own at this point. However, I am provided with the opportunity to continue this process as fear returns. I repeat by increasing the white light around me with my intention and feeling my love for the Divine and all fear disappears. Apparently, the love for the Divine is the antidote for fear, at least in this process. I consciously decide that "class" is now over as I can only process so much of this experience at one time and let Spirit know that my intention is now to return to my physical body and so I do. I feel safe, relaxed, warm and cozy in my bed and in a total state of awe and wonder.

Two quotes come to mind as I was lying awake, absorbing the experience I had, and both quotes are from the infamous Yoda in the movie Star Wars. The first quote that comes to mind is Yoda telling Luke Skywalker, "Do or do not. There is no try." There was no effort or trying required when accessing this Quantum field of infinite possibilities. There is a very delicate dance and a fine line between trying to make something happen and allowing something to happen using your intention and then aligning with the Divine to co-create. When we are "trying" to make something happen beneath that there is a small fragment of doubt that it cannot be done. When we truly believe something is possible, there is no doubt. We simply know that it's possible. And when we come to believe and connect with a power greater than ourselves, the Divine, we then have access to infinite creative ability. In the second quote that comes to mind is when Luke says, "I cannot believe it." and Yoda replies by saying, "And that is why you fail." It comes to my understanding that the only real essential part of transforming the singing bowl or glass of water, in whatever way I wanted to, was the fact that I believed I could do it. The belief was paramount, above all things. Perhaps the teaching of Yoda can make us believe in things and the powers of the Divine, which we can't see or understand.

My next profound experience happens at a meditation retreat in Toronto in September of 2018. I am sitting in one of the many daily meditations, with 1100 other participants in the room. The breath work prior to the meditation allows for Kundalini energy to rise effortlessly and the energy in the room is beyond words. I decided this time to sit at the back of the

CAROL COWAN

room, to be away from friends, so I can feel truly able to let go.
I am sitting on the floor for this meditation and the Divine
gently communicates to me that during this meditation I
should be prepared to fall forward and land on the floor but
that I will be ok and safe. I respond with a willingness and
openness to whatever happens. Then I am shown, in my
mind's third eye, a rectangular chocolate chip cookie at the end
of a buffet table on a white plate. The cookie is so strange
because it's a rectangle and it makes no sense to me
whatsoever. I am shown every subtle detail of this strange
cookie, so much so, that it totally captivates my full attention.
Then suddenly, out of nowhere, the cookie disappears into
pure vibration and the Divine whispers "There is no cookie
Carol. None of this is real. It's just vibration. It's all pure
vibration. It's all a dream. You're dreaming Carol." I then
experience energy moving through my body so intensely that I
lose the ability to hold myself up and I burst into tears of joy.
I fall forward in my seated position, but I don't hit the floor.
Because there is also no floor. The floor has also turned into
pure vibration at that point and then "I" disappear into
nothingness, falling through the floor. It is beyond words. The
Ego sense of self disappears, and it feels like death if I had to
guess what death feels like. At the same time, it is the most
beautiful, quiet, serene experience ever. There is an experience
of being in a void of nothingness that feels like pure infinite
unconditional love. I have no concept of how long I was there,
in that position, because in that state there is no time. It felt
like floating forever in this vast space of infinite potential
where everything and nothing exists at the same time.

112

Eventually, everyone in the room is guided out of the meditation by the teacher, and I come back to my physical body and sit up with tears of joy and love stained on my face.

Of course, this doesn't happen just once during the week of the retreat. It happens again, 2 days later. Sitting on the floor, deeply in a state of meditation, I see in my minds third eye, a shopping cart in the corner of a room. Strange, right? It gets better. One wall in the room is fake green grass which, just like the other meditation, feels very strange and out of place. I swear I must be in the twilight zone or something. I'm focused intently on every subtle detail of this shopping cart and the grass wall when I suddenly feel the presence of the Divine within me and all around me. Then the Divine pulls the grass wall off like wallpaper. And what is behind the wallpaper? An infinite black space. A void of pure loving energy that is everything and nothing at the same time. Then "I" move into this infinite space and disappear into pure vibration myself, resting in the arms of the Divine, once again.

On the final day of this retreat, the group goes into meditation with a focus on the Pineal Gland, also known as the third eye, or center of intuition in yoga. During this meditation, I feel my body melt to the floor that can only be described like the witch who melted to the floor in the Wizard of Oz. All that is left after I feel my body disappear is my conscious awareness. My consciousness is then free to move around the room as I've left my body now. I am floating above all 1100 people sitting in meditation in the room now. There is a distant horizontal line a few feet above everyone's head that distinguishes dense physical form from the vast energy and space above them. To my right is a giant keyhole, that would be large enough to walk through if I was in physical form at that time. And beyond that keyhole is another keyhole and another keyhole and another. In fact, it appears as though there are infinite keyholes as if two mirrors were facing one another. I know that I can move through that keyhole if I like and enter another dimension, or any number of dimensions, as they are all occurring at the same time which is the present moment. I have a thought about whether I can come back or not if I travel to these other dimensions and with that little bit of doubt and concern, the keyhole disappears in front of me and I end up back in my body. I am left with the feeling that traveling to other dimensions is possible, without a doubt. I know that there is so much more to explore and that those opportunities are always available to me. Needless to say, such profound experiences of meditation can change you forever. You just can't go back to living life like you used to.

I am left in a state of amazement after each of these experiences. It was truly invaluable to have the experience that our reality is not as solid or concrete as it appears but rather a web of vibration that connects us all. It was incredible to be shown that the universe just consists of waves of possibility that collapse into particles of experience called "our life" when we become the observer of those waves. And that if we can strengthen our belief about our own power and the power of the Divine, then we are able to shape and contour these waves into the particles that we desire to see and experience in our lives. This means that if we can learn to melt metal, shape it into that which we desire, and then reshape it again, that anything is truly possible. This means that to connect with the Divine then is to merge with the infinite power of the Divine. This also means that our reality is pure vibration at the most subtle level and that by shifting our vibration from the inside out, we can then have an influence on our external reality. Through practice, we can develop and strengthen our belief and our ability to influence our own experience of the world. To manifest that which we desire and co-create with the Divine intelligence that gives us life. It is an art and a discipline to learn how to move into a state of pure vibration so that we become infinite potential in the moment. Moving into a state of meditation where the mind is quiet and we lose track of time, space and the physical body is the state in which we become pure vibration with the ability to connect with our own Divine potential.

Another way of thinking of this process is that we must become conscious and aware and fully present in the moment so that we may allow the Divine to express itself through us. In fact, it is our purpose in life to become a vessel through which the Divine can create and express itself. When fully present in the moment the mind is like a window or screen into a realm that is completely infinite. There are no boundaries to the realms of consciousness, they never end, and they contain absolute infinite possibility. We all share the same consciousness, but we are in separate bodies, here and now. This "consciousness" is also known as the Divine or God. Your "unconscious mind" is more powerful than any supercomputer, more knowledgeable than any academic, more completely full of accurate information than anything you can possibly fathom, and it's possible to harness the incredible energies of consciousness in many ways.

In fact, everything we do is a matter of harnessing and interacting with Consciousness, the Divine or God. All things in nature and in the world are expressions of consciousness. Take some time each day to sit in complete silence and do absolutely nothing. Simply still your mind and sit quietly and try to connect with the silence you feel around you. Hear any sounds that emerge from that silence, but simply sit and experience. Allow thoughts to come and go and be aware of them but not attached to them. This is one way in which you can experience the true nature of consciousness. It is the silent infinity from which all emerges. This Divine essence is your true essence.

In this quiet place when we connect with the Divine we begin to harness the power to have influence over our destiny. And if it is true that we have influence over our lives because everything is just subtle vibration that responds to our intention, then what would you create in your life? If it is true that in your current waking reality you possess the ability to connect with the Divine which has infinite, creative powers, what experience would you desire to co-create with the Divine? Could we agree that if the Divine is everywhere, always, all-knowing, all-powerful, that we also have access to these powers simply by connecting to the Divine? We simply need to be open to connecting with the Divine that is already within us and all around us.

And if this is all true…that this interconnected web of vibration is available to you, to become your conscious playground of infinite creation as you connect to the power of the Divine, would you start to say that anything is possible?

And if you came to believe that this is the absolute truth with every fiber of your being then…

What would you do?

Who would you want to be?

What would you want to experience?

What emotions would you want to feel on a daily basis?

What sort of life would you consciously create?

If you have not asked yourself these questions yet, then now is the time to do so. Now is the time to shift your awareness and attention to your ability to create what you desire in your life and ask the Divine to dance with you in the process of creating this. Like a blank canvas, we can create the life that we desire, with a little help from the Divine along the way. As we focus our mind's attention on what we would like to create and allow the Divine to arrange some synchronistic events for us, we are able to have an influence on these waves of possibility and transform them into a new reality.

And what if this is not your current belief or understanding? What if your faith in the Divine waivers at times? What if you still think that your reality must be difficult to change because you have not yet had the actual experience of it being a web of vibration and infinite possibilities?

Ask yourself for a moment, what would be the worst thing that would happen if I believed in the power of the Divine with unwavering faith? What would be the worst that would happen if I came to believe that my reality is not solid, but rather changeable and that I indeed have the power to change it via my consistent thoughts? This is a great responsibility to accept, but once you do there is infinite power to consciously create our reality with the Divine. Shifting from feeling like you are at the mercy of life to becoming a conscious creator is a challenging endeavor. But, again, once we're on the awareness train, there's no getting off. Once you realize the infinite power that lies within you already, and that has always been within you, there is only a heartfelt desire to consciously create and manifest. There is only a longing to connect with the Divine and become the vessel through which the Divine co-creates. Once you have a taste of this magical experience, life will never be the same. And all it takes sometimes is to have one synchronistic event or one miracle happen for us in order to begin to develop that belief.

The other good news is that a belief is simply developed by repeating a thought over and over again. And as we repeat a thought, over and over, the brain begins to develop neural pathways and strengthens those neural pathways every time we think that thought. Then this set of neural pathways becomes the filter through which we see and experience our world. Those who consistently think thoughts of how miraculous the Divine truly is will often find themselves blessed with magic and miracles. Those experiences of magic and miracles then reinforce the neural pathways in the brain as they get fired again, which then, in turn, strengthens the belief in the Divine even more. Those who waver in their belief of the Divine, often find that they receive inconsistent guidance from the Divine. At this point, it is essential to focus one's attention on the effortless unfolding of synchronistic events in order to strengthen one's belief system. Perhaps it is just that simple. That the external world we experience every day is simply a mirror for our belief systems. And if that's the case, then what better way to live life than by repeating thoughts and believing that we are supported by this infinite Divine organizing power and that we can co-create that which we desire in our lives with limitless possibilities. What better way to live life than to repeat thoughts that the universe is flexible, malleable and changeable once we are able to access this infinite field of vibration. And so, to strengthen that belief, repeat that thought. Repeat that thought, and then repeat that thought again. And as you repeat that thought, and strengthen that neural pathway in your brain, it must be reflected in your reality. You will begin to sense the Divine with you at all times, supporting you and arranging things for you in your favor in your life. You will begin to feel the infinite love that the Divine has for you and learn to influence your life by commanding the waves of possibility to collapse into particles of a beautiful, wonderful, amazing life that you've decided upon.

This process of thinking a new thought and strengthening a new belief does take time and concentrated effort. Learning to dance within this interconnected web of the Divine Universe can feel sticky at first. You might fumble around, trip and fall, and get back up. You might feel in total flow and connected with the Divine and then fall back to feeling like you're struggling. You will have moments when you feel deeply connected as you have experiences where you realize the interconnectedness of all things as a synchronistic event occurs and then disconnected as you have experiences of feeling lost, waiting for Divine guidance. There will be times where life feels effortless as you have an experience of manifesting an experience because you've been thinking a repeated thought and feeling that it was possible for you. And, of course, there will be times when your belief in the Divine waivers as something does not manifest as quickly as you would like it to or how you pictured it initially. This is all part of the process as you cross from the realm of doubting to the realm of having complete and total faith in the Divine. The most important part is to enjoy the process and journey along the way. Stay present with the process.

To be more specific, here are some dance steps to practice in order to experience the interconnected web of the Divine Universe:

Step One: Daily "Dissolving" Meditation

Step Two: Choose to see the Divinity in others

Step Three: Observe the Divinity in nature

And to elaborate on these steps....

Step One:
Daily Dissolving Meditation.

In order to connect and merge into the vibration of the Divine that surrounds us, we must surrender, melt and dissolve the awareness of the physical body. We must dissolve the outside edges of the physical body in order to merge with the Quantum field of infinite possibilities that is all around us. If we attempt to change our external reality with the conscious mind, we will experience difficulties. The conscious mind is the screen or veil through which we see our external world. This veil is often layered with limiting beliefs that restrict our infinite ability to create. And so, one approach to lifting that veil is to enter into a state of meditation in which we bypass the conscious thinking mind and access subconscious mind wherein lays infinite creativity. If we are to dance with the Divine and co-create our life with the Divine then we must access the field in which the Divine is patiently waiting for us with loving, open arms.

Prior to practicing this meditation, it is beneficial to understand the different brain wave states that occur during the process. Eventually, you will be able to recognize when you shift into various brain wave states. In fact, you already move through these varying states every day.

"Beta" is the brain wave state where you feel alert, you are concentrating, thinking or analyzing. You would experiencing a Beta brain wave state when you are active in a conversation or focused while playing a sport for example. The "Alpha" brain wave state is a more relaxed state. This Alpha state is where you would access creativity and awareness.

This is not quite a state of meditation but rather an experience of being fully present in the moment. The "Theta" brain wave state is a deeply relaxed state of meditation where you can access intuition and experience a feeling of expansion. You may feel a sense of floating as the outside edges of your body begin to disappear. The "Delta" brain wave state is one of detached awareness, deep restorative sleep, and healing. Your brain cycles through these states daily as you awake in the morning, move into Beta, stay in Beta most of the day while you're working. Slip into Alpha during the boring afternoon meeting when you feel as though you need a nap. Move back up to Beta as you talk about your day with your partner at home that evening. Slip back into Alpha as you relax when bedtime approaches. Then dive into Theta and Delta as you move into a deep sleep. You also continue to cycle through these different brain wave states when you sleep at night and move into states of dreaming and back to deep sleep.

So, for those who believe that they "cannot" meditate, the good news is that your brain already knows how to get there! As you begin to practice the Daily Dissolving Meditation you are essentially consciously guiding yourself from a Beta brain wave state, into Alpha and then into Theta. When we are in a state of Alpha but more so in Theta the door to the unconscious mind opens. This is where we connect with the infinite organizing power of the Divine and access our own creativity. This is where we melt into the interconnected web of the Universe. How do you know when you're in a state of meditation? You will likely forget about your environment and where you are in space. You will also lose track of time and long durations of meditation will feel short. You will also lose track of your physical body as you dissolve and connect with the space around you.

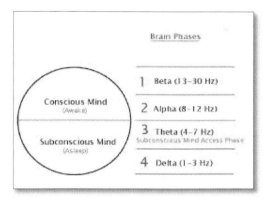

Dissolving Meditation:

Find a comfortable place to sit with your spine tall if possible. It may be best for this process to sit in a chair with both feet planted on the floor. Let go of "trying" to make something happen and instead be open and curious about the process, without any expectations or obligations. Notice the difference between forcing yourself to relax and allowing yourself to relax. Once you close your eyes down, begin by feeling the sensation of where the feet come to meet the floor, and where the floor comes up to meet your feet. Just sense and experience that sensation for a few moments. Now, feel the sensation of where the backs of your legs come to meet the chair and where the chair comes to meet the backs of your legs. Just stay with that sensation for a few moments. Notice the connection. Notice where your hips come to meet the chair and where the chair comes to support your hips. Feel that sensation. Good. Now feel the sensation of where the chair comes to support your back and where your back comes to meet the chair. Notice points of connection between your back and the chair and notice the parts where there is no connection. And then feel the sensation of the head floating comfortably above your shoulders and neck and how it connects with the rest of your physical body and the area around it. Now imagine that there is a beautiful, bright, white healing light that's coming down from above and in through the crown of the head. This beautiful white light is now moving down through your physical body and filling you up. This healing light can dissolve any pain or discomfort in the body. Move this white healing light down through the head, the neck and then down both your arms. Move this white light down through your entire torso and into your low back and hips. Then, move this white healing light down through both legs and into your feet. Now imagine that this white light is moving out through the soles of your feet and into the earth, connecting Heaven above you and the Earth below you. This continuous flow of white light healing energy is moving through you and dissolving any pain, any stuck energy or negative emotions, simply surrendering it to the earth beneath you. Let anything you want to let go of simply dissolve into the earth now. And now, imagine that the white light is beginning to leak out of each one of your pores and beginning to surround your entire physical body. Imagine this white light surrounding you, in all directions and simply dissolving into the area around you. Now, take a moment to become aware of the space above the crown of your head. Notice the space between the crown of your head and the ceiling and notice the space between the ceiling and the crown of your head. Just notice. And now, notice the space between the front of your body and the wall in front of you and notice the space between the wall in front of you and the front part of your body. Just notice. And now, notice the space between the back of your body and the wall behind you and notice the space between the wall behind you and the back of your body. Just notice. And now, notice the space between the right side of your body and the wall on your right and notice the space between the wall on your right and the right side of your body. Just notice. And notice the space between the left side of your body and the wall on your left and notice the space between the wall on your left and the left side of your body. Just notice. And now, notice the space between the soles of your feet and the earth beneath you and notice the space between the earth beneath you and the soles of your feet. Just notice. And now, notice the space all around you, all at once. Good. Now allow yourself and the outside edges of your physical body to simply dissolve into that space. Good. Notice the sensation of yourself expanding into the space around you and relax deeper and deeper. The more that you relax the more you feel yourself dissolving into the space around you. Join with the interconnected web of the Universe that is all around you and then feel the subtle vibration of this web. Connect with the unconditional love of the Divine that is all around you. Rest here in the arms of the Divine.

When you are ready, notice yourself back in your physical body and notice the density of your body. Bring your attention to the outside edges of the body and where you are resting in your chair. Receive a long deep full breath in and a long slow breath out. Invite yourself to come back now feeling centered,

relaxed and with an overall sense of well-being. Open your eyes, looking down first and slowly turning your gaze ahead.

Practice this Daily Dissolving meditation at least once a day for approximately 20 minutes. If 20 minutes seems too long you can simply start with 5 or 10 minutes because some meditation is better than no meditation. The key to success and starting a new habit of doing this is to make the meditation the utmost priority of your day. It may even mean giving up some sleep, but you will be in a relaxed state of Theta while you are in meditation which provides the ability for the brain and body to rest and restore anyway. This will essentially become your way of strengthening your connection to the Divine so that you can live in a state of feeling guided and as though you are co-creating with the Divine. Once you feel the essence of this interconnected web and the loving support of the Divine you will look forward to doing this Daily Dissolving meditation in order to continue to cultivate that relationship.

Step Two:
Choose to see the Divinity in others

Once you come to fully understand the vastness of this interconnected web you will begin to see others differently in life. Instead of seeing them as separate from you or noticing their "faults", you will instead recognize them as the part of the same interconnected web and therefore part of you. You will comprehend that any negative thought you have about another person is really only harming yourself as you are both parts of the same web. You are both made of the same vibration and therefore are forever intertwined at a deeper level. And the Divine loves each one of us on this planet unconditionally. And so, when you find yourself judging another person, or meet someone that triggers a negative cord within you, pause for a moment and ask the Divine to help you see this person through the eyes of unconditional love. Invite yourself to see this other person through the eyes of the Divine and to see the true essence of who they are beneath all the conditioning and programming that they've been receiving since arriving in physical form this time around. Ask yourself to see them as part of the interconnected web of the Universe instead of separate from you. This approach is also best applied when you meet others that you feel are superior to you in some way or that you admire because of how amazing they are in your eyes. Remember, again, that they are also an aspect of you and connected with you via this web. They are also loved unconditionally by the same Divine Universal energy that loves you. Whatever your reaction to others you meet along your path, simply make a conscious choice to recognize the Divinity within each one of them and know that we are all intertwined and entangled in this web together.

Step Three:
Observe the Divinity in Nature

Again, as your awareness expands to encompass the completeness of this interconnected web you will also come to see yourself as an extension of nature and nature as an extension of yourself. You will notice the grace and ease with which nature transitions through the different seasons each year and then begin to recognize the Divine life force energy that resides in all parts of nature that sustains itself through the transition of the seasons. Paralleled with that, you will notice the Divine life force energy within yourself that also sustains its presence as you transition through the ups and downs of different stages in life. As you notice the Divine essence within you and notice the same essence within nature you will likely begin to make a conscious choice of how you interact with nature and how you treat all living things on this earth. They are all part of this same interconnected web and seeing nature as an extension of yourself means you are more inclined to treat it with the same love and respect that you treat yourself with. Once you recognize that you and nature are all part of the same web you will also begin to flow more with the rhythms of nature and move through challenges in life as though they are cycles of essential growth. From the perspective of the Divine, which constantly desires to create and grow, the cycle of spring, summer, fall, and winter can be seen as the process of birth, life, death, and rebirth. We as humans with our Divine essence, also transition through this process of birth, growth, decay, and rebirth as we move through challenges during developmental periods in life as well as when we move through numerous reincarnations. Being able to recognize the Divine as the thread that intertwines among all things in nature and in us will also provide one the ability to see the magnificence of this interconnected web.

And now, let us understand the importance of practicing connecting with the Divine and practicing having faith!

CHAPTER 5:

DANCING DAILY – PRACTICE, PRACTICE, PRACTICE

So how does one become a better dancer? Imagine for a moment that you go to dance practice at the studio every day and you practice the same salsa dance turns and foot placement patterns over and over. You will move through the stages of learning, from being unaware of the movement to focusing on the movement, to the movement being automatic for you. The one and only thing that can move you through these stages will be the act of practicing the dance. As you practice the turns or foot placement patterns over and over you begin to strengthen a pattern in your brain as neurons begin to wire together on a consistent basis. The more that you fire that neural pathway the stronger it becomes. Eventually, when you're on the dance floor the firing of the neural pathway becomes automatic as the body and brain remember what you're asking it to do. This is the point at which the dance feels like it is "automatic", and you may even experience a state of being in total flow when you're on the floor.

The most fascinating part that the world of neuroscience is recently discovering is that you do not necessarily even need to be in the dance studio, on the dance floor practicing in order to be strengthening this pattern or neural pathway. It has become evident that using the power of our own mind, concentration, and focus, we can close our eyes and repeat such dance turns or foot placement patterns repeatedly using our imagination and mental imagery. The simple act of imagining yourself repeating the dance moves in your mind actually fires and strengthens the very same neural pathway in your brain. Therefore, you can be sitting on your couch at home with eyes closed and using mental imagery to repeat the dance moves in your mind over and over again and start to become a better dancer. Now, of course, nothing is more impactful than the actual practice of being on the floor, with or without your partner, engaging in the experience, in order to become more proficient at the movement. However, this understanding of the brain's ability to strengthen a neural pathway by thought alone is vital to the process of developing a new belief and shifting your reality. This means that by simply turning your attention inward, withdrawing from your external environment, you can literally create your own inner world. At this point, the mind and body will respond as though you are engaging in that activity in the moment.

What is most important to understand about this process is that by practicing any thought or repeating imagery in your mind, you begin to fire neural pathways in the brain and that the body will respond emotionally as if that event is occurring in the present moment. The subconscious mind is always in the "now" which means that it only knows the present time, as opposed to the past or future. A study was conducted by Australian Psychologist Alan Richardson where he split people into three groups and tested each group on how many free throws they could make. After this, he had the first group practice free throws every day for an hour. The second group just visualized themselves making free throws. The third group did nothing. After 30 days, he tested them again. The first group improved by 24%. The second group improved by 23% without touching a basketball! The third group did not improve, which was expected. So, if you were replaying dance steps in your mind, two weeks before you were to do a performance for a Christmas party, for example, the mind and the body, neurologically, physically and emotionally would respond as though that event was happening right now. And if the thought of performing a dance in front of a few hundred people made you nervous, and you began to imagine yourself walking out on stage to begin dancing, you might feel your heart rate increase, blood flow increase, and breathing rate increase as adrenaline releases into your blood stream. Even though you are only imagining this event in your mind, weeks prior to it actually happening, the body responds as if it's happening "now". If you truly enjoyed performing a dance in front of others, then you would experience a feeling of excitement or confidence as you went through the same imagery of walking out onto the stage in your mind. So, the lesson here is that if you are worried about a future event or feeling excited about a future event, the body is responding emotionally and physically as if that is happening right now. At the same time, the brain will also be strengthening that neural pathway of worrisome thoughts or confident thoughts, depending on your thinking pattern, as well as strengthening the corresponding emotions to those thoughts. Hence the importance of choosing your thoughts wisely and consciously!

As we come to understand the significance of the fact that the subconscious mind does not know the difference between what's real and what's imagined, we begin to recognize just how powerful we really are and take on the responsibility of transitioning to becoming conscious creators in our lives. Now, the subconscious mind and the body have always been responding to the thoughts and images you have in your mind, but you may or may not have been aware of those thoughts or consciously made effort to redirect them. Perhaps you can recall times you have thought an anxious thought or held a stressful image in your mind, and your body responded with stress hormones, whether or not that stressful event was happening in your environment at that particular moment or you were just imagining it. At the same time, you can likely recall thinking a calm thought or holding a relaxed image in your mind, real or imagined, and your body responding to that with the engagement of the relaxation response in the body. So, the more you practice any thought or imagery in your mind, the more you fire the same neural pathway in your brain, the stronger that pathway gets. This means that the corresponding emotions also become stronger and stronger. The question is...what consistent thoughts and emotions have you been practicing?

Anything that you practice or repeat over and over becomes strengthened within your belief system and within the vibrational energy field that surrounds you. This means that consistent thought patterns, daily behaviors, or feeling certain emotions, become like an ingrained pattern in your energy field. Now, this may be a good thing as perhaps you have developed a thought pattern that increases your self-worth and self-esteem and has created wonderful experiences in your life. Perhaps this may sound like "bad news" if you've been practicing a thought, behavior or emotion for a long time that has not been serving you or loving to you. However, the good news is that the subconscious mind is only ever in the "now", so you can start a new vibrational thought pattern, a new emotion and a new behavior now and simply continue to strengthen that pattern over and over from this point forward. At the same time, it is also vitally important that you become aware of and stop thought patterns that are not serving you in your life. You are likely already aware of your consistent thought patterns, habitual behaviors and frequently experienced emotions as they are going to be mirrored for you in your everyday life. And if you are not aware yet, your external environment is the first place to look as it is a direct reflection of your underlying belief system which is connected to the thoughts you have been thinking on a regular basis, which are, of course, also intertwined delicately to the frequent emotions you experience and behavioral patterns you engage in.

Let's look at this process of creating a pattern in another way. Take a moment to imagine an old black vinyl LP record. If you're not quite sure what that is, you are likely then from the generation that can just Google an image of it or ask your parents what a vinyl record is so that you can form an image of it in your mind. Now, imagine all the grooves in the record being analogous to thought patterns in your mind. As you think a consistent thought over and over, it's like digging a

135

deeper and deeper groove in that record. So, imagine digging a groove just on the outer ring of the vinyl record with a negative thought that is also connected to a negative emotion. For example, let's say the thought is "There's no way I can achieve that. I'm not good enough. Maybe they can do it, but I can't." The associated emotion connected to that thought is frustration, resentment or perhaps jealousy. This, of course, leads to behaviors such as avoiding situations that challenge you or not taking chances for new opportunities. And every time an event occurs in your external environment that reflects your current level of skill or knowledge, it triggers you to think that thought and feel that feeling. This, in turn, strengthens that energetic vibrational pattern around you and deepens that groove in the record. Now, imagine picking up the needle on the record player and moving closer towards the middle of the record and placing it down on a new groove. This new groove represents your new thought which is "I am worthy of all I desire in this life, just like everyone else." You consciously repeat this thought daily and it begins slowly to elicit an emotion of hope, confidence or joy. You then seek out situations within your environment that allow you to practice a new skill or apply for that new job. And as you successfully achieve applying that new skill or you are hired for that new job, your automatic thought is that you are in fact worthy of what you desire, and you continue to deepen the new groove in the record. This then becomes your new vibrational, energetic pattern of worthiness and feeling good enough.

Initially, when you move the needle over from the old negative groove to the new positive groove in the record and you start to think a new thought, the new thought might not "sound true" to you whereas the old thought still does. This is only because the old groove is much deeper than the new groove. You simply had practiced the old negative thought more often and for a longer period until it became believable to you. This means that practicing the new thought over and over until it becomes believable to you is essential. In fact, the easiest way for this new thought to become anchored into your subconscious is to move into a relaxed state of meditation first and then imagine scenarios in which you would feel worthy and think the associated thoughts of worthiness. When you move into a state of meditation you bypass the critical thinking, conscious mind and move directly into the subconscious. But, like anything, this new pattern of thought requires practice!

You will also notice the temptation for the needle in the record to slide and slip back into the old groove in the record. Again, because this old groove and pattern are deeper, the needle is going to be drawn back in that direction. Even though you may not like the negative feeling of being frustrated or resentful, it at some level feels familiar, comfortable or easy for you, or it just feels like "that's the way things are". Sometimes the negative feeling, although unpleasant, is more comfortable because it's all we've ever known so it's almost difficult to trust the new positive feeling and belief about being worthy in this example. The process of changing a thought pattern and, therefore, a pattern of emotions and behaviors, is uncomfortable and so it's essential to "get comfortable with being uncomfortable". If you remain with the uncomfortable new thoughts and emotions long enough, eventually they become your new way of being and your new normal. So, when you feel the needle slipping back towards the old groove in the record and you notice that thought that attempts to remind you that "you're not good enough to achieve something," it's vital that you pick that needle back up, over and over again, and move it to the new groove in the record and repeat the thought that you are worthy and that it is possible for you to achieve what you desire. Practice the new thought, the new emotion, and the new behavior until it becomes your new normal. Eventually, the new groove becomes deeper and deeper and the old groove begins to fade away. The longer that you keep the needle playing the song in the new groove in the record the sooner that you forget the words to the old song.

You will know that you're in the process of changing when you feel uncomfortable. This feeling of discomfort will eventually become your new way of confirming that you're on the right track. Instead of avoiding the discomfort it will be a signal to you that you're engaging in a new thought or behavior. Now if you'd like to get an idea what change feels like and begin to encourage your brain to change in new ways, you can start with something simple. For example, you can start by brushing your teeth with your non-dominant hand. This will feel awkward and require your full attention in the process of something you probably do without much thought on most days. You likely engage in the behavior unconsciously most days which means that brushing your teeth with your left hand, if you would normally use your right hand, will require conscious attention and encourage your brain to become more malleable in the process. You can also try moving your kitchen garbage to the other side of the room for example. As you move the garbage from under the sink to the other side, just observe how many times you automatically reach to place the garbage in the old location, before remembering that you've moved it. Count how many times if you like, just for fun. If you're reaching for the old location you're likely operating from "autopilot" or unconsciously at that time. Notice that eventually, you will reach to place garbage in the new location automatically after the brain and body establishes a new pattern of movement for something that you probably do every day. These simple tasks can help you to train your brain to be more flexible but also to help you realize just how much attention and focus is required to change a pattern! Eventually, the new groove becomes the dominant pattern, whether that's a way of thinking, or a way of brushing your teeth or a way of moving to put something in the garbage.

139

Similarly, the more that you practice anything the more that it becomes part of the vibrational pattern that surrounds you. This is also known in the Yogic Tradition as a Samskara or an impression embedded in the subconscious mind. A Samskara is similar to the idea of the groove in a record as it is akin to generalized patterns, a way of being or repetitive ideas or actions that make up our general conditioning. The more often a samskara, or pattern, is repeated the more it is reinforced. As a result, reinforced Samskaras can make it more difficult to resist or break free of the pattern. The best way to get out of an old pattern that you feel stuck in is simply to create a new one! We must find a way to create a new thought, a different thought or more positive thought, regardless of whether or not our current life circumstances are reflective of that thought. Samskaras can be either positive impressions that support us in a peaceful way of life or negative impressions that cause pain or suffering in our lives. Samskaras are universal and simply part of this human experience, but we also have the capacity as human beings to use our frontal lobe to redirect our mind's awareness and attention in order to create new samskaras. The function of the frontal lobe is to carry out higher mental processes such as thinking, decision making, and planning. The negative samskaras are what hinder our positive evolution and spiritual growth and development. The process of working though samskaras and transforming them is part of the spiritual path. Most people, when they first step onto a yoga mat in a studio are not aware that this is part of the yogic path. The shifting and changing of one's samskaras also results in changing one's vibrational energetic pattern, and as the energetic pattern changes, one's reality changes. Your reality changes, because you changed your vibrational pattern from the inside out, not the other way around. So, as you vibrate at a more positive, higher vibration, you can create and invite in more positive and uplifting people, places and things in your life. Of course, the Divine is always there to assist you in this process.

Now, let's examine the practice of connecting with the Divine. If it is true that the more we practice certain thoughts, the more that it strengthens our belief systems, imagine what your life would look like or be like if you focused your thoughts on the Divine energy that sustains life, this energy that is all-knowing, all-powerful, within you and willing to support you at all times. Your thoughts about the Divine and the capacity of the Divine to assist you on this journey called life are like grooves in that vinyl record. Take a moment to examine the current grooves in your record when it comes to your beliefs about this Divine Source.

Is there a groove in the record at all? Are you undecided about whether the Divine actually exists and if miracles can happen for you?

Is there a negative groove in your record? Was an authority figure's negative belief regarding the Divine ever passed on to you?

Is there a positive groove in your record? Do you already believe in the Divine and perhaps already had past experiences of small miracles or synchronicities happening for you? Would you like to strengthen this belief?

The most beautiful part of this process is that in order to feel closer and more connected to the Divine we can simply practice and repeat thoughts that strengthen this belief system. We can deepen the positive groove in the record that has embedded past experiences of feeling a Divine connection. For example, remember a time in your life when you felt like your life was in flow. Remember a time in your life when you felt like there was something greater than yourself that was guiding you along this path called life. Recall an event where you felt that there was some sort of Divine intervention. Tell the story again of that occasion when a difficult situation worked out better than you could have possibly imagined. You know...the time when everything in your life seemed to be falling apart or something "negative" happened to you. And then a few months or a year later you were able to see that situation in a totally different light. You could see it as some sort of Divine intervention, gently nudging you to move forward and make a significant change in your life. And looking back you can see how it was all happening "for you" and your soul's evolution and not "to you" in a negative way. Recall the time when you experienced a synchronistic event such as thinking of a friend that lives in another country on the other side of the world and then coincidently getting a phone call or email from them just shortly after. Think of the time when you experienced something challenging in your life and you closed your eyes tightly and prayed to God or the Divine for the situation to resolve completely and then surprisingly or unexpectedly the situation changed and vibrated right out of your life. Remember the sense of wonderment the first time you read about someone else having a "spontaneous remission" from a serious health ailment or prognosis of only a short time to live. Remember the goosebumps and chills you felt the first time you read a story about someone else's near-death experience and how it changed their life and what your reaction was when they explained what "heaven" is like or what it's really like on the "other side." Think about how many times you've experienced that feeling of Déjà vu or meeting someone that you immediately connect with so well that your souls must have been together in a previous lifetime. Perhaps you've had a dream at night that actually came to be true sometime later and so it must have been a premonition instead of just a dream. There is an infinite number of ways in which the Divine shows up for different people in their lives but most of us, at one time or another, have had some sort of interaction with the Divine. If we have not had the personal experience ourselves, we have been amazed by the stories of others as they explain their interaction with Divine source energy.

Now, the more that we focus our mind's attention on the Divine and its infinite organizing power, the more that we strengthen our belief of the Divine and deepen that groove in the record. And the more that we strengthen that belief, the more that the Divine shows up to dance with us and support us in our lives. And the more often that we allow ourselves to be led by the Divine on the dance floor of life, the better we get at following Divine guidance and living life in flow. And the better we get at

living life in flow, the easier life gets and the more magic and miracles we have the joy of experiencing every day.

So, to strengthen that belief and connection with the Divine and to deepen that groove it is essential to practice, just like practicing any other skill! Remember that this process can be a delicate dance. It's a bit of an art. It requires balance and letting go and trusting which can be challenging for most people. Trusting the guidance of the Divine will be positively reinforced the first time you let go and a solution is provided for you in a wonderfully unexpected way. The joy that is experienced in that moment will become a positive experience for you and likely encourage you to repeat the process. And as you realize that letting go and asking the Divine for help was one of the best things you could have done in that situation, your brain will release positive endorphins, deepening the groove in the record, strengthening a positive neural pathway which means you are more likely to ask the Divine for help the next time you're in a challenging situation.

Keep in mind that this practice of connecting with the Divine is not so that we can experience and live a "perfect" life as all of us will experience challenges in our lives, this part is inevitable. In fact, this experience here on earth is more like school and probably the toughest school around. The soul typically comes to school here on earth to learn and to experience life. The process of life allows us to come face-to-face with the negative grooves in our own record or our past samskaras. Each day we have the opportunity to be fully present with life, fully present in the moment. As we live fully in the present moment, we are no longer operating from past conditioning or samskaras. The more we stop playing the negative groove in the record and get out of the pattern of a harmful Samskara, the more freedom we feel and the more opportunity the soul has to simply experience the beauty of the present moment as it is no longer clouded by the past. Now, you may find a way out of one groove in the record or clear one samskara as you create new healthy patterns instead, only to find that you are met with another challenging experience in life. This challenging person, place or thing seems to bring up some other pattern or groove within you that you didn't even know you had because it must be that old! And yet, you start again. You always have the opportunity, when fully present in the moment, to not operate from that past samskara or pattern. In fact, this is a very important part of the process of spiritual enlightenment. So, it's not that connecting with the Divine daily will absolve you of any and all problems in life, forever and ever. It does, however, mean that you will have a deeply rooted groove in your record which represents your belief system that the Divine is there to support you and guide you as needed to live life more in flow. This belief that you have in the benevolence of the Divine will allow you to respond to the challenging circumstances in life with grace and unconditional love. You will find yourself blessed with synchronicities, magic, and miracles when you were not able to see a possible solution to a problem just days before.

And so here are some dance steps you can take to practice connecting with the Divine:

Step 1:
Identify exactly how you get into "groove" with the Divine

Everyone connects with the Divine in a different way and experiences the support and guidance in a unique way. Remember the feeling when you were totally connected with the Divine and everything seemed to flow easily? Think about a time when you experienced a coincidence or synchronistic event.

If you don't have one you can go back to the Synchronicity Journal that you've started or recall someone else's experience. Whatever it is, the most important part is that you know how and when you feel most connected to the Divine so when you're not in the groove with the Divine you know how to get back into the groove! It is essential that you cultivate the awareness of when you are not in flow or feeling a connection to the Divine and take time to step back and reconnect. Perhaps it's time with nature or time in silence or going to church. Once you know how you get into a groove with the Divine you can practice that method again and again. And repeat and practice that whenever possible.

Step 2:
Feel deep hearted gratitude daily

Feeling gratitude for everything in your life is one of the best daily practices you can engage in to most effectively connect with the Divine and to create a life where you truly feel blessed. Every day, whether we realize it or not, we are practicing a pattern of thinking which is then producing a corresponding pattern of emotions. Take a moment to become aware of the emotions you experience on a regular basis and then notice the thoughts connected to those emotions. Perhaps you frequently experience a range of positive emotions or negative ones. Consider how often you feel a deep sense of gratitude for all that you have in your life. If you don't currently feel gratitude daily, then it is something that you can turn your conscious awareness towards and practice. Focus your attention on things in your life that you can feel grateful for. You may feel a sense of lack in your life currently if there is something that you believe to be missing in which case some might say it's difficult to feel grateful. However, this is the most important time to feel gratitude. When you focus on what's missing in your life, you create more feelings of lack because that's how the thinking and feeling cycle works. These thinking and feeling cycles are what creates the vibration that surrounds you and reflects your current reality back to you. Similarly, when we have thought patterns and emotional patterns that radiate a vibration of gratitude daily, then our reality will reflect those back to us. The most difficult part is breaking the pattern of feeling lack and practicing a pattern of feeling gratitude instead.

So, if your current life circumstances make it difficult for you to feel grateful, you have two options. First, you can find the smallest thing in your world to feel grateful for and focus your attention on that, which may be as simple as the fact that you're breathing or that you have clothes on your back. Second, you can close your eyes, withdraw from your external environment and create within your own mind a situation or circumstance that you can feel grateful for. When practiced daily this exercise has the power to draw into your life that which you desire. The mind does not know the difference between what's real and what's imagined. The body and subconscious mind simply respond to the images replayed in your mind whether that's negative or positive. So, take time out of your busy day, close your eyes, let your imagination run wild and let the feeling of gratitude flow freely. Let that feeling of gratitude run so deep in your veins that it eventually pours down your cheeks in the form of tears and expands your heart center large enough to fill the entire room. Then, wait and watch how the Divine so eloquently brings you more opportunities, situations, and things in your life to feel grateful for.

Step 3:
Pray and talk to the Divine often

The actual act of prayer is a method of communicating with God. Most often we pray to God for what we want or need in our lives such as better health or safety. We may also give thanks to God via prayer for the current circumstances in our lives. Another way of understanding the act of prayer is to recognize that as you shift your mind's attention to your belief in something greater than yourself you are first and foremost strengthening that belief. Perhaps you pray to God or the Divine or another Higher Power of your understanding. Regardless, the act of prayer is important. As you shift your mind's attention to the Divine and give thanks, you are changing the vibration that surrounds you because all thoughts have a vibration. Your belief that the Divine can provide this for you will strengthen the vibration around you.

So, to say that the act of praying changes the circumstances in your life is not quite as accurate as saying that the act of praying changes you and your vibration allowing collaboration between you and the Divine to change things together. The act of praying or talking to the Divine changes the way you look at things in your environment. Although it may seem that praying leads to change in your external world, it is producing miracles within yourself, changing your reality from the inside out. This, of course, means that daily prayer is recommended in order to co-create consciously with the Divine. You are, in fact, praying most of the time anyway as your consistent thoughts are always producing the vibrational bubble around you. This means that the act of worrying is akin to praying for that which you're worried about to occur in your life. Hence the importance of noticing thoughts which are connected to a feeling of worry, redirecting those thoughts, and asking the Divine to take away the feeling of worry and to replace it with Divine wisdom, truth, and unconditional love instead. Then give thanks as you trust and know the Divine can assist in creating what you do desire to have in your life and shift your mind's attention to images of what that would look like. And let the Divine handle the details of how or when that happens...

Step 4:
Use mental imagery to co-create your desired life with the Divine

Sounds simple enough doesn't it? Just mentally rehearse what it is that you desire to create in your life then let go and allow the Divine to arrange synchronistic events in your life that are in vibrational alignment with that. The most challenging part for most people is to make the practice of mental imagery the most important part of their day, every day. Most often we are too busy dealing with current situations in our life which inhibits the ability to pause and mentally create a new potential future. So, if you can find a way to make your meditation and mental imagery the main priority of your day, every day, then you are on the road to co-creating a future with the Divine that is truly only limited by your imagination.

This practice of mental imagery combined with gratitude is a very powerful one. After attending my very first yoga retreat at Pura Vida Spa in Costa Rica, I was literally transformed in the most benevolent way. After spending a week there and having life-changing experiences and enlightening moments, I decided to come home and become certified as a Yoga Instructor with the intention of bringing as many yoga students back to this retreat center so that they might also have a similar experience. My goal at the time was to host my own yoga retreat within a year. Within 6 months of returning to Canada, I was certified as a Yoga Instructor and started teaching as many classes as I could. I then started planning, organizing and marketing my first Yoga retreat to be held at Pura Vida Spa. My intention in my heart was purely to provide a beautiful and enlightening experience.

Every night when I went to bed for the next six months or so, I would close my eyes, relax my mind and my physical body and begin to imagine sitting in my favorite yoga hall at Pura Vida Spa in Costa Rica. I would mentally rehearse walking up the three steps into the hall, rolling out my yoga mat to sit down, looking out the patio windows at the beautiful view, noticing the bright orange color of the flowers, watching the wind blow the curtains slightly, and feeling the warm breeze on my face. I would feel the sense of calm and peace that the yoga hall provides. I would then hear the footsteps of my yoga students entering the hall to join me. One at a time, they would roll their mats out and sit down together. Eventually, there are twenty beautiful souls sitting in a circle with me all quietly enjoying this peaceful place. I imagine making eye contact with each of them and offering them my deep-felt sense of gratitude for being there. I thank them for trusting me enough to come all the way to Costa Rica to deepen their yoga practice and connect with a deeper part of their soul. I am so grateful that tears are literally rolling down my cheeks as I say, "thank you for coming". These tears eventually roll onto my pillowcase. Although I'm lying in my bed, at home, in Canada, my brain and my body emotionally believe that, in that moment, I'm in Costa Rica experiencing this. Again, the mind does not know the difference between what's real and what's imagined and feeling the emotion as if it's happening now is the most important part of mental imagery.

And so, I practiced this very same mental imagery every night for months and months. On occasion, I would come across someone negative who would ask me what I would do if I didn't get enough students to host the retreat and my response was that I never even thought about that or worried about it. I just would refer to the cancellation policy if needed and went on with my mental imagery. And, with a little help from the Divine of course, randomly and coincidently, students would sign up for my yoga retreat one by one. My hope was to have just twenty students join me for my first retreat and on the day, we arrived there I was blessed to have twenty-three, lovely, dedicated yoga students with me. Just a year and a half after being at Pura Vida Spa, and within my first year of teaching yoga, I had co-created a successful yoga retreat with the help of the Divine. As we all sat down together in the yoga hall for our "welcome meeting", the curtains blew in the warm breeze, the hall felt quiet and peaceful and everyone rolled out their yoga mats one at a time. Sitting in a circle together, I had the opportunity to thank each one of my students for joining this retreat with me, but this time, as the tears poured down my cheeks, they actually landed on my yoga mat in Costa Rica instead of my pillow, at home in Canada. The whole event turned out just like I had imagined it over and over…. only better as my heart center felt even more gratitude for each of them and for the Divine.

So, when you engage in the practice of mental imagery it is essential to incorporate the correlating emotions and feel gratitude before the event actually exists in your life. You are accessing the subconscious mind during mental imagery which primarily understands images, emotions, and sensations. For example, imagine palm trees blowing in the wind and waves lapping up on the beach (image). Feel the grains of the sand between your toes and the warmth of the sun on your shoulders (sensations). Feel the gratitude in your heart as you take a moment to appreciate nature surrounding you (emotion). Remember to incorporate as much detail as possible during your imagery and repeat daily!

Step 5:

Read about other's experiences of connecting with Divine

When you take the time to read about someone else's experience with Divine intervention it truly has the potential to strengthen your own belief in the Divine and therefore provide you with invaluable faith. The act of having faith and worrying are quite similar. Both require that you believe in something that has yet to happen or occur in your life. Faith means believing that the Divine has something wonderful in store for you, perhaps just around the corner, while worry is believing that the worst is about to happen. Either way, you're strengthening a positive pattern or negative pattern of thinking in your mind. So, reading books that focus on faith in the Divine can provide you with hope, inspiration and a deeper understanding of how the Divine works in wonderful and mysterious ways. There are countless books written on miracles, Divine interventions, spontaneous healings, near-death experiences, and heaven. Find one that calls to you, resonates with you and brings you back into that place of trusting in something greater than yourself that is always on your side. When you're having a day that you feel worried or unsure about your future, redirect your focus and take the time to pick up one of those books that strengthen your faith instead.

Step 6:
Spend time with nature and time in silence

Nature seems to know what it's doing, all the time, without any question. Flowers know when to bloom, the leaves on the trees turn color at the perfect time and the ocean's tides change in perfect rhythm. There is an infinite, unseen intelligence that has tremendous organizing power which is ensuring this process called life continues to unfold. This infinite power is also known as the Divine and this infinite power also exists within you as you are part of nature. This infinite power exists everywhere, in all things, and is more powerful than you could imagine. Your only responsibility is to connect with it, acquiesce to it, learn to dance with it and create your life in alignment with it. Spending time with nature is one of the easiest ways to connect with this Divine essence as it can restore us to our "natural" state of being. Nature is always growing, changing in cyclical patterns and ever unfolding in an effortless way. When we spend more time in nature, we become more like it. The essence of the Divine can easily be seen in nature and therefore it is easy to begin to vibrate with the rhythms of nature, the closer you are to it. Take time to sit by a stream or river and watch how the water easily flows over and around the river rocks. This is akin to our ability to live life in flow and maneuver around perceived obstacles in life. Take time to observe the graceful unfolding of flower petals over time and the progression from a tiny bud to a beautiful blooming, wonderful smelling blossom. This is akin to our ability to transition from keeping ourselves small in life to allowing our soul's natural talents to be nurtured and shared with the world.

Then take some time to go to the top of the highest mountain you can find and listen to the stillness and silence there. The top of the Rocky Mountains in Alberta and British Columbia would be appropriate for this example. If you desire to know what the Divine sounds like, you will find it there. You will find the same stillness and silence in your heart that you find at the top of those mountains should you choose to challenge yourself with the hike. The silence is a sheer, quiet bliss like nothing else on the planet. The significant silence at the top of such a magnificent mountain can only provide you with faith in something greater than yourself as only something Divine can create such beauty. And if you can't make it to the top of a mountain, know that this silence also exists within you. By quieting your mind, taking time out of your busy day, and sitting in meditation you can also connect with the Divine. Although many people find silent meditation difficult because their mind is racing around in circles with unrelated thoughts, with practice, it is possible to find the stillness within. Initially, as you allow yourself to simply be in your seated posture, you will observe the thoughts. Eventually, with patience, you will find a space between the thoughts. With time, that space between thoughts begins to lengthen and you find silence. This silence is your opportunity to connect with the Divine because this silence is the Divine. This silence is where we can hear the deepest desire of our soul and listen to Divine guidance. Finding this stillness and silence requires patience and practice but is worth every drop of effort for that glimpse of Divine connection.

Step 7:
Spend time with other people who have similar beliefs in the Divine

By spending time with other people that have a belief in the Divine we can begin to learn from their experiences and strengthen our belief in the possibility of Divine miracles as well. When someone tells you a story of a synchronistic event that happened in their life, take the time to listen with awe and wonder. When someone you know tells a story of a small miracle that occurred, ask them how they know that the Divine or God was the unseen element that allowed that miracle to transpire. If you spend time with people who are strong in their faith in the Divine, then you can be rest assured that the days you experience doubt you can call them and they will be able to remind you of all the support you have received from the

Divine up to this point in your life and help you get back into groove with the Divine. And as you develop trusting relationships with these people, you will also likely find yourself being supportive of them too. Perhaps you will be the one reminding them of the Divine guidance they've had in their life when they have a day of feeling disconnected. Seeking out others who have a deeper relationship with the Divine can also open your mind to the infinite possibilities that are truly possible.

If you happen to lack friendships or relationships in your life with people that have a connection to the Divine, there are a few places where you're likely to find them. Although they are all around us, you're likely to find deeply spiritual people attending church, practicing yoga or meditation, visiting temples, going to motivational conferences or spending time in nature. Simply remaining open and receptive while spending time in places where spiritually aware people congregate can bring about new relationships. You can also ask this magical Divine guiding intelligence to show you the way to meet new people that are also connected and spiritual. Then do your best to trust the Divine to lead you in the right direction to meet those people that you best resonate with.

Step 8:
Repeat your stories of connecting with the Divine as often as possible

If you are blessed enough to have had an interaction with the Divine, whether that's a synchronistic event, gentle guidance or a small miracle, the best thing you can do is tell the story to as many people as you feel comfortable telling. Every time you tell that story, the deeper the groove gets in the record and the more you strengthen that pattern in the vibration of energy that surrounds you. Tell the story from beginning to end, laugh about how it turned out to be better than you could have ever imagined and repeat how grateful you are for the experience. Over and over, tell your story about how much you feel connected to the Divine and how magical your life feels when you continue to focus on that connection. Be prepared because some people may look at you strangely or not know how to relate to you. Keep in mind that this just means they lack a positive "groove in their record" when it comes to dancing with the Divine. Just remind yourself that this person has yet to take any dance lessons, let alone practice dancing with the Divine, and therefore does not have a neural pathway, thought pattern or belief system within them that allows them to relate to you and what you're saying. Therefore, it's more valuable to surround yourself with people that have similar beliefs in the Divine. Regardless, the more that you repeat your stories of connecting with the Divine, the more that the Divine wants to serve you and flow through you to create and manifest.

Step 9:
Try dancing with a partner as a method of learning to "let go"

If you find it difficult to let go and surrender to the will of the Divine, the act of dancing with a partner who is leading you is one way for you to experience what it is like to let go and be led. There are, of course, several different ways but let's first examine this option of dancing. When you are holding your dance frame, relaxed and focused, your partner who is leading can support you, carry you, and signal to you every step of the way, where to go and how to move with the music. If you resist and try to control the process, the whole experience of being in flow falls apart and both people experience difficulty in moving in rhythm with the music. However, if both people agree that one is leading the dance and the other is following, and the leader is confident, and the follower trusts the leader, then the dance is magic on all levels. If you are open to the experience, taking just a few Ballroom or Latin dance lessons with a qualified instructor can allow you to have this blissful experience of trusting and letting go.

There are other opportunities to have this trusting experience with someone and come to know what it feels like being "led" while you relax and "follow". Any activity that involves you letting go of control and trusting another human being can facilitate this trusting experience. It might initially feel like going back to being a child again, which can feel vulnerable at first and perhaps even a little scary. Think about a parent holding their child in the water as they learn to swim. Imagine a parent helping a child learn to ice skate for the first time. Imagine a parent holding onto the seat of a bicycle as their little one begins to balance and pedal. The child, at some level, knows that the activity may be potentially harmful if they fall but they trust their parent 100% to support them, guide them and ensure their safety. If you can learn to trust the Divine in a similar way, then you're on your way to living a Divine life.

Surrendering your life to the Divine means following the Divine's lead without knowing exactly where you're going. Just like when you are dancing the Tango, you may be required to move backward at times without any awareness of where you might be heading. You've just got to trust that your partner knows where they're going. It's also essential to wait for Divine timing without knowing when you might experience guidance or the manifestation of your focused intentions. Similarly, while on the dance floor, you patiently wait, without anticipating, for the next subtle lead from your partner so you know where to go next. The idea is to be in a neutral and grateful state of being, expecting a miracle, without knowing exactly how the Divine will provide for you and meet your needs. The simple act of trusting the Divine's higher purpose for you without understanding the circumstances is one that can lead to a miraculous and fulfilling life.

Remember, you get to decide "what" you would like to experience in your life by repeatedly feeling the emotion of what it would be like to have that in your life. However, you do not get to decide where, when or how it will happen. In fact, by letting go and allowing the Divine to arrange the details, the outcome is guaranteed to be better than you could have possibly imagined. Instead of trying to resolve the issue from your own mind, let go and allow of the infinite mind of the Divine to show you the way. Besides, the Divine has infinite organizing power and all-knowing intelligence. Really, can you think of anyone else that you'd rather be co-creating your life with?

Step 10:
Read the book "The Spontaneous Fulfillment of Desire" by Deepak Chopra

This book outlines how meaningful everyday coincidences are and describes how they are essentially a manifestation from the field of infinite potential. There is a specific meditation practice that is outlined within in order to come into alignment with the Divine and experience more synchronicities in your life. Practice the daily meditation with devotion and dedication, then wait and watch how life unfolds with coincidences in the most magical way.

CHAPTER 6:

DANCING WITH GRACE AND EASE – GETTING IN RHYTHM AND STAYING THERE

The hardest part of the process of learning to dance gracefully with the Divine is the "learning" part because it only happens over a period of time with consistent practice. We can sometimes get into a rhythm with the Divine but maybe have a hard time staying there. Again, think about any skill you've learned in your life, whether it was riding a bike, starting to swim or trying rock climbing. The first part was always the hardest. The beginning stages are the ones where we want to give up and go back to our old patterns of thinking or past ways of being. Learning to let go and allow the Divine to lead us in our purpose in life is no different. For example, you might let go for a short period of time, experience some Divine guidance or intuition, feel amazing as you tell others, but then get frustrated or impatient when your desire to manifest something else is not happening in the time you thought it would. You then lose your faith in the Divine. It will likely only be temporary though, as you find it is harder and more challenging to try to make things happen yourself. And so, you acquiesce and surrender to the Divine again, trusting in that which you desire will happen in the perfect way, in the perfect time, in the perfect place. The ability to trust and have faith is

163

the key but, like trees blowing in the wind, trust can waiver sometimes. If we were to examine what is happening in the brain when trust waivers, we'd see we've just gone back to an old thinking pattern and the corresponding emotional pattern of doubt. We've stumbled back into our belief system that we must do everything ourselves and that life must be a struggle. The needle has slipped from a positive groove in the record where we have trust and faith in the Divine to a more negative groove in the record that feels like doubt or frustration. The only way to strengthen a belief is to think the thoughts and feel the corresponding emotions related to those thoughts. This means you've got to find a way to get back into rhythm with the Divine and get back in the groove. You've got to find a way to think the thoughts and feel the emotions that you felt when you were dancing with grace and ease and letting the Divine lead you.

Awareness will be your key to getting in rhythm with the Divine and staying there, particularly the awareness of your thoughts. Now, being aware of each of the 60000 to 70000 thoughts you have in a day is not realistic, but there is likely a pattern of thinking that occurs since close to 90% of your thoughts are the same as the day before. Your key will be to just become aware of the pattern of thoughts that lead you back into the negative groove in the record where you lose faith in the Divine or feel frustrated or disconnected. You cannot change what you are not unaware of, so it's important to take the time to become conscious of the thoughts you think when you feel any negative emotions, particularly if you feel them often. Now, once you become aware of the thoughts that you think when you're in that place, you can begin to interrupt the pattern. Before the needle slides off the record and down into that negative groove where you lose faith in the Divine, your responsibility is to notice that thought and redirect it. You know that if you follow that thought it will result in you feeling a negative feeling and not flowing with Divine grace and ease. The sooner you can interrupt that landslide of thoughts in that direction, the easier it is to redirect them to a more positive groove of thought. Remember the snowball example: If you follow a negative thought pattern it can become a larger and larger snowball, or even a snowball rolling downhill, gaining speed and size simultaneously. Now, try to stop that snowball! It's not easy because of the momentum it's been gaining. So, the moment you notice a negative thought, you can acknowledge it, remain unattached to it and then consciously choose a thought that is more in line with the positive thought groove in your record. An amazing and unique ability that we have as human beings is that we can be conscious of our thoughts and can redirect them. Cultivate and use this ability as often as you can. The good news is that once you get back on track with the positive groove of thoughts, the easier it is to stay in the groove and flow easily with the Divine. Similarly, that snowball you start rolling can represent a positive thought. Allow yourself to roll that positive thought down the hill and watch that snowball gain momentum and size. Your blissful connection with the Divine and starting to feel like you're flowing through life will become a direct reflection of this.

So, how can you redirect the thought pattern once you become aware of it? Typically, what works for most people is positively affirming what they want to feel like or repeating a positive affirmation or statement. A positive affirmation, for example, might be "I accept myself just the way I am" or "I am so grateful that I now have a career that I enjoy", or "I am so happy to be in this relationship". You would need to repeat that positive affirmation enough times so that it feels true for you. It is essential to understand that if you state a positive affirmation but deep inside feel different or feel that it's not true for you, that you may actually be doing yourself a disservice. The thought and the feeling must correlate for your communication with the Divine to be clear. Otherwise, you're sending mixed messages to the Divine and your reality will continue to reflect that back to you. The trick is to use a positive affirmation that has a positively anchored emotion connected to it already. A positive affirmation that was, perhaps, true for you on your best day and that emotionally feels true for you no matter what else is going on in your life. Perhaps it's a positive belief about yourself or the world that even in challenging times feels true for you. That is the positive affirmation that you want to turn your attention to when you want to redirect away from a negative thought pattern.

What is another way for you to redirect a negative thought pattern and get back to dancing with the Divine? Mental imagery and visualization can be very effective in shifting your state and the vibration that surrounds you. Take the time to close your eyes and be still inside as you relax your mind and go through a series of images, sights, and sounds in your mind that produces a positive emotion. Again, your mind does not know the difference between what is real and imagined, it simply responds emotionally and chemically to the thoughts and images replaying in your mind. Just like the positive affirmation though, it is essential for the mental imagery to be in alignment with a positive feeling. If you try to visualize something you want in your life but currently only feel the lack of it, then you are again sending mixed signals. You must find a way to feel the emotions of that situation or experience as if they already existed in your life. Approaching the practice of mental imagery with a sense of fun and playfulness as opposed to taking it too seriously can also be helpful. The trick is to get beyond the thinking mind that might say what you're visualizing is not possible. Once you do, the subconscious mind has no limits and you can practice feeling the emotions of a fulfilling life beyond your wildest dreams. Using mental imagery, you can lift your energy and shift your vibration to consciously co-create a life with the Divine that becomes a direct reflection of those positive emotions. Once you learn how to use mental imagery to get into a state of flow with the Divine you will be able to redirect your thoughts more easily.

So, getting in rhythm with the Divine and staying there is truly a delicate dance. We cannot force the Divine to dance with us and we cannot force ourselves to be in a flow state. Getting into a state of flow is a state of mind. A state of mind that you cannot force to happen and, in fact, *trying* to get into a state of flow, ironically enough, can inhibit the flow. Think about an activity you were so captivated by or engrossed in that you completely lost track of time. Recall an occasion where nothing distracted you and you were fully present in the moment with that activity or person. Being in a state of flow requires that you "allow" yourself to be in flow. You simply move into it rather than think about moving into it. You find yourself in it. You recognize that you've been in flow minutes or hours after you've been there and lost track of yourself, where you are or what time it is. When you experience a synchronistic event, a small miracle, intuitive guidance, or messages from the Divine, you are in a specific flow state. You are open and connected with the Universal web at that point. The idea is to stay in that flow state and maintain that connection for longer and longer durations so that you cultivate a stronger and stronger connection. And when you recognize that you're out of flow and not connected with the Divine, to stop what you're doing and take the time to reconnect, either via shifting your thought pattern or using mental imagery. Being connected with the Divine to consciously co-create your life must become one of your essential priorities each day. Once you come to understand the power of the Divine and the interconnected web of the Universe, you won't want to let your thoughts wander to a negative place or linger in any negative emotions as you will recognize the value and importance of staying connected and focused in a positive place.

We are always dancing within this interconnected web of the Divine Universe every day, but most people are dancing without the skills or awareness of the proper steps to take and why. In fact, you have always been a part of this interconnected web and always will be. You just may have not been conscious of the fact that you were even within this web, let alone aware of the fact that you can begin to work within this web and with the Divine to consciously co-create your reality. Once you come to acknowledge this interconnected web and open your heart to the Divine, there's no turning back. There may be days where you wish you could fall back into being unconscious and unaware because being a conscious co-creator of your life requires energy and focus. However, wanting to forget about this magnificent force in life would be like saying you want to forget how to ride a bike or forget how to speak your native language. Once you've had a taste of dancing with the Divine, you'll never want to take your dance shoes off again!

Now, this interconnected web of the Divine Universe is always reflecting back to us our deeper-rooted belief system, our vibrational thought pattern, and consistent emotional patterns that we experience. Therefore, to change our reality or reshape our lives, we must vibrate at a different emotional frequency by thinking different thoughts and shifting our belief system about ourselves and the world around us. In this case, we must first take some more advice from the wise, old Yoda!

"You must unlearn that which you have learned." - Yoda

Essentially, this means that we must become aware of our thought patterns, emotional conditioning and belief systems that are no longer serving us in life. Then we must unlearn those patterns, habits, and beliefs before we can cultivate new habits, patterns, and beliefs. And guess who is going to assist you through this entire process? You guessed it…the Divine!

The true art of this process is getting in a rhythm and staying there. The magic happens when you can cultivate a new way of thinking along with new positive emotions and stay in rhythm with that new way of life. This new way of being or feeling will initially feel awkward, new, different or uncomfortable but that's a good thing because that means you're changing. This is the time when the Divine will arrange people, places and things for you that you least expect. And if you stay connected to the Divine in this conscious co-creation process, you can continue to strengthen this new way of being. Your old way of being and your old belief systems that were not serving you will attempt to draw you in and pull you back into old habits. Again, to "unlearn" this way of being, it is necessary to stop the thought pattern and behavior pattern associated with that old way of being. The moment you become aware of an old pattern attempting to creep back in, you can ask the Divine for help to redirect your thoughts, emotions, and behaviors. When your mind is open, quiet and relaxed, you may even be able to feel or hear the whispers and nudges from the Divine that will help you stay focused on your new path.

Let's examine this process a little more...

Step One:
Acknowledge this Interconnected Web of the Universe

You may or may not already have an understanding of the interconnectedness of all things in this Universe. For some people, seeing one's self as separate from this Divine Universe can lead to a lack of faith in something greater, lacking meaning in life or a negative world view. For others who have contemplated or developed a belief in the interconnectedness of all things, they often experience a sense of purpose, a sense of being supported by something greater and a more positive world view. Acknowledging this interconnected web is vital if one is to become a conscious co-creator of their life with the Divine because it is part of the basis from which the practice extends. One must be connected to all things around them and connected to something greater such as the Divine, in order to break old beliefs and instead create a life that one could only dream of. The simple act of experiencing miracles, coincidences and synchronistic events means that you are interwoven with this connected web of the Universe. How else would such serendipitous moments occur?

In order to acknowledge this complex web that we live within, we can simply pause and take a moment to ponder the wonders of nature. One can wonder about how nature operates with such a delicate balance and in such an intricate way. Think about how important it is for bees to cross-pollinate in order to sustain a wide variety of crops. Take a moment to contemplate how the gravitational pull of the moon has the capability to change the tides of the ocean. There is an underlying intelligence that so gracefully allows one season to turn into the next, year after year, without fail. Nature does not operate within a vacuum but rather as a complex and interconnected system. We, of course, are part of nature and connected to this system without a doubt. We, as human beings, have influenced nature, and have been affected by it as well. We are not separate from it and, in fact, we depend on it! We support one another at the same time by breathing in the oxygen that trees produce, and, in turn, we sow seeds in the earth to produce more food. It's a very delicate and complex system that we are part of and the Divine is the source energy that supports all living things in this Universe and connects us all. The Divine is the underlying, infinite intelligence that is the source of creation and the organizer of the natural cycles of life.

See and acknowledge how you are connected to this infinite Divine source every day. The source energy is all around you. You can see it if you look closely enough in nature. Observe the water flowing in a stream that gracefully caresses its way around the rocks in the middle. Look up at the stars and moon above you on a calm, clear night. Take the time to watch the effortlessness of a beautiful sunrise or listen to the sounds of waves lapping rhythmically on a beach. You can also see this source energy if you look closely enough and deep enough into someone's eyes, in a quiet moment. You can literally see their soul. Take a moment to look deep into the eyes of a loved one, a newborn baby or even a pet and, in that moment, you will see yourself. You will see the interconnectedness of all things. You will be able to feel the Divine essence that lives within us all. Then, and only then, can you even begin to comprehend the vastness of the Universe and that infinite love that the Divine has for you. Observe the present moment and you will inevitably start to feel the Divine source supporting you and the unconditional love it has for you. You will see how you are a very important part of this complex, interconnected web of the Universe.

Step Two:

What belief system have you developed about yourself or the world? What beliefs do you need to let go of?

This interconnected web is a part of you and you are part of it. This web is vibration at the most subtle level and so are we. So, if our thoughts and emotions are also held at a vibrational level then what we experience in life is a mirror of our most consistent thought patterns, emotions and belief systems. All throughout our lives, we are dancing within this vibrational web. This vibrational web is essentially responding to our vibrations which means that we can shift and change our lives and our reality by changing our thoughts, emotions, and beliefs. We can change our belief system and begin to vibrate at a different level and therefore have a new, different interaction with this vibrational web. This is a process of changing your life from the inside out, not the other way around. Change your belief system and watch how the vibrational web around you responds and shifts.

Take some time to think about what patterns you seem to experience in life. What pattern do you experience in your career or in relationships or with money, for example? What do you know for sure about the world and your experience of it? Is the world a supportive place or difficult place? What do you believe about the Divine or God or Source Energy? The patterns you experience in your life are in fact a reflection of your underlying belief system. Some of your belief systems may be very supportive and beneficial to you. Keep those beliefs strong and firm! Examine if there are any belief systems you have that are not serving you. Perhaps you hold a belief that you are not good enough, not deserving, not worthy or not lovable? Typically, these are the most common for people. We must first acknowledge the underlying belief system that is not serving us if we are to change it. Typically, it's not easy to look at this part of ourselves, but acknowledging your belief system puts you in the place of power because once you recognize it you can change it. This is also the part where we ask for the assistance of the Divine. Once you become aware of your belief system that is not serving you in a beneficial way in your life, it's time to acknowledge it and change it. One way to facilitate this process is to bring the belief to mind, write it down in your journal so you can see it outside of yourself and then ask the Divine to erase this pattern of thinking and belief system. Ask the Divine to replace this belief system with Divine wisdom, knowledge, understanding and unconditional love. Ask the Divine to see yourself and others and the world through the loving eyes of the Divine. "Divine, let me see the world through your eyes". As you are quiet and listen with an open heart and mind, you may hear and come to understand a new thought, idea or belief system. When you do, ask the Divine to help you repeat this new thought or belief system repeatedly until that becomes your new way of thinking and seeing the world. Take the time to write down this new thought and belief system next to your old one in your journal. You can even cross out the old belief system. Once you know and become familiar with the belief system that is not serving you, the continuous work is to become aware when thoughts come up related to that belief system and redirect them, repeatedly. Asking for Divine intervention as needed of course.

Step Three:

What new beliefs must you come to realize? Choose to focus your attention on that which you desire to cultivate in your life.

So, what is the opposite of the belief that is not serving you? If you believe that you are not worthy, then the opposite would be that you are, in fact, worthy of all good things. In the eyes of the Divine, you are always worthy. If you believed that you are not good enough the opposite of that would be feeling that you are good enough, just as you are. Again, in the eyes of the Divine, you are always good enough just as you are. So, what new beliefs would be more beneficial for you in your life? Take a moment to step back from your life and everything that's happened up to this point. Imagine that, in this moment, you could just start over and develop a new set of beliefs about yourself and the world. What would you want to believe? What would your life look like if you believed that? Stretch your brain to think differently! Think of someone in your life that obviously has a different set of beliefs than you because there is evidence in their life that is a reflection of that. For example, if you want to come to believe that you're worthy of a loving, healthy relationship, then think of someone in your life that already has that and ask yourself what belief must they have about themselves and the world that creates that? If you want to come to believe that you deserve a better life or are worthy of earning more money, then think of someone that already lives that life and ask yourself what consistent thoughts must they think every day? What beliefs must they have that I don't? If someone else on this planet experiences that which you desire to have in your life, then that means it's possible! Take the time to write down these new thoughts and beliefs. Take the time to ask these people, if you know them personally, what they believe and what are their consistent daily thoughts. They believed it was possible for them and so it can be possible for you too, via shifting your beliefs. Keep in mind that even if no one else on the planet has experienced what you desire to create in your life that doesn't mean it's not possible. It just means that no one has ever thought that way or believed that it was possible before. This is how every great invention was ever developed.

Now, as you shift from your old beliefs and come to realize new beliefs that are in alignment with what you desire, keep in mind that this is a process that can take time. It's important to ask yourself, *what is the opposite of my current belief?* This way you can identify what you would need to think in order to create change in your life. What happens for most people when they first think the opposite is a reaction inside that feels like that's not possible for them or that it may be possible for other people but that will never happen for them because of their past. There will likely be several reasons why your mind will tell you it's not possible for you to live this way. Don't believe everything you think! This would be a normal reaction based on your identity which is an accumulation of all your past experiences. Therefore, it can be a stretch for the mind to consider the opposite belief. In this case, it can be more helpful to ask yourself, "I wonder if I could begin to believe something a little different?" Start by simply shifting the belief a little bit. Think of what the opposite belief would be to your current negative belief and then find a belief that's halfway in between. For example, if you believe that you're not good enough, it may feel unnatural and untrue when you try to believe that you incredibly worthy and more than good enough, the first time you try to think that way. It may be more beneficial for you to first start by simply wondering if you could feel like you are good enough. Start by contemplating areas of your life where you do feel good enough and then ask yourself if you could apply that same feeling of being good enough to the other areas of your life where you don't feel good enough. The most important thing is that you come into alignment with your new belief and find a way for it to feel true for you.

Again, one of the best ways to do this is to ask the Divine for help in this process of transition. Ask the Divine to help you to think a different way or see the situation differently. The Divine, which is all-knowing, has access to infinite ways of allowing your life and situation to change. Your task is to open up to that possibility and allow the Divine to guide you to new situations, people, places and things so that your life can change to come into alignment with your new set of beliefs. The challenging part is shifting your focus and your attention towards that which you desire to cultivate in your life and think the thoughts related to that. Allow yourself to believe that it's possible for you and that this Divine infinite organizing power loves you so much that it only desires to assist you in creating that. The Divine desires to create and requires you to become an open vessel to allow for creation and change. Ask yourself, "What would the Divine think?" or "What does the Divine believe is possible?" and feel how your brain stretches into a new way of thinking.

Finally, when you come to realize the new beliefs that you would like to have, you've written them down, and you've asked for Divine assistance, put them up somewhere that you can see them. Put them up around your home in a place where you'll see them every day. Whenever you notice yourself going back to your old beliefs or old ways of thinking, these postings of your new beliefs will be a constant reminder of the new you and your new beliefs.

Now, during this process of change, which can be challenging due to falling back into old ways of being, it is recommended that you allow the Divine to carry you during the tough times. After all, that's when we need the support of the Divine the most. And so, the question is, how exactly do we know when we are dancing with the Divine?

CHAPTER 7:

HOW TO KNOW WHEN YOU'RE DANCING WITH THE DIVINE UNIVERSE

The Divine is our invisible partner in this dance called life. It is only when we allow ourselves to be led by this Divine partner that we can be taught certain steps!

You must first come to believe that this Divine loving energy is always here with you and available to support you, guide you and carry you. In fact, it always has been and always will be. The Divine knows everything about you. By everything I mean your wishes, thoughts, worries, hopes, dreams, desires and secrets. This Divine energy loves you unconditionally and only desires to guide you and dance with you till the end of time. This Divine energy is always with you because it experiences life through you. It is important to be open to support and guidance in your life and to ask for help when you need it. Just the simple act of asking for help can change everything for you. The Divine only waits patiently and respectfully to assist you but it does require a little letting go on your part. It will feel like going with the flow or going with the current or…. like you are being carried. The most graceful description of this experience can only be conveyed by the remarkable poem written by the one and only Mary Stevenson:

Footprints

One night I had a dream--
I dreamed I was walking along the beach with the
Lord
and across the sky flashed scenes from my life.
For each scene I noticed two sets of footprints,
one belonged to me and the other to the Lord.
When the last scene of my life flashed before me,
I looked back at the footprints in the sand.
I noticed that many times along the path of my life,
there was only one set of footprints.
I also noticed that it happened at the very lowest
and saddest times in my life.
This really bothered me and I questioned the Lord
about it.
"Lord, you said that once I decided to follow you,
you would walk with me all the way,
but I have noticed that during the most troublesome
times in my life
there is only one set of footprints.
"I don't understand why in times when I needed you
most,
you should leave me."
The Lord replied, "My precious, precious child,
I love you and I would never, never leave you
during your times of trial and suffering.
"When you saw only one set of footprints,
it was then that I carried you."

And so, once you decide to follow the Divine, once you give up your troubles to the Divine and become open to receiving the assistance or guidance in new and various ways, you will be lead through this beautiful dance called "life" in the most effortless way, with comfort and unconditional love. As you open your mind and your heart to receive this support you will begin to feel deeply worthy and perfect just as you are. You will no longer see yourself through the eyes of judgment or the lens of the ego but rather you will see yourself through the eyes of the Divine which will allow you to know that feeling loved and being joyful is your birthright. The feeling of how deeply loved you are by the Divine is almost indescribable because it's so incredible. You will come to realize that you have been worthy of this profound love your entire life and it will shatter any former beliefs you had to the contrary.

So, what does it feel like when you're not dancing with the Divine? And what does it feel like when you are dancing with the Divine? Let's start with how to know when you're not in flow with the Divine. The main purpose of becoming aware of when you're not connecting with the Divine is primarily so that you can notice when you're in that state and pull yourself out. Once you recognize that you're not in flow, and your emotions and thoughts related to that state, then you can stop what you're doing and take the time to get back to dancing with ease. Typically, if you're experiencing a negative emotion you're not in flow at that moment. Any negative emotion can be a sign of not being connected to the Divine. It might feel like you're resisting against life or trying to force an outcome. It might feel like frustration or struggling. It might feel like you're lost or confused with what choice to make. Emotions such as anxiety, fear, anger, shame or guilt are all states of not being in a state of effortless flow. When you're judging another harshly, feeling resentment or experiencing doubt or despair you also know that you are off the track at the moment. When you're not dancing with the Divine, you might feel like you're trying too hard or that you're attempting to make something happen. You may experience the sensation of going against the flow or paddling upstream. It may even feel like you've hit a brick wall sometimes. This is the point where it's important to stop, take a break and go find your dance shoes so you can get back in flow!

Keep in mind that experiencing a negative emotion is not necessarily a bad thing, in fact, negative emotions are a necessary thing for everyone at some point in their life. It would be unrealistic to expect someone not to experience sadness at a funeral. It would be unrealistic to not feel fear if you found yourself in a dangerous situation. It would be unrealistic to expect someone not to experience hurt when a relationship ends. These negative emotions are meant to be temporary, while experiencing the situation, but not meant to become a part of our everyday life. It means that staying in that state for extended durations means a longer length of time of not being connected to the Divine. In fact, in that moment that you're experiencing that negative emotion, you can ask the Divine to help pull you out of it. The trick is to remember to ask for help in that moment because chances are that asking for help in that moment may be the last thing you think of doing. It can be difficult to shift your mood or emotions when you're entrenched in them. Hence, the importance of asking the all-powerful and all-knowing Divine essence to support you at this time and transform the negative emotion into a higher state of wisdom, knowledge, understanding and unconditional love. Ask the Divine to resolve the situation in a way that is beyond your understanding. Open yourself up in that moment and receive a deep full breath in and a deep full breath out to transform and shift the energy of the emotion. Open your heart and mind to the Divine in that moment to bring you a sense of peace and calm as you return to a neutral state.

The length of time that you're not dancing with the Divine and sitting on the sidelines of the dance floor of life is up to you to a certain degree. Sometimes, you may find that when you're in a place or a situation in your life that you don't want to be experiencing that it feels easier to stay stuck in that place. When you feel stuck is another indicator of not being in flow with the Divine. As you sit on the sidelines, in distress, your feet could feel like two left feet or the equivalent of cement blocks. The irony is that the times when we need to lighten up and dance the most can be the hardest time to do so. The good news is that you don't have to jump out of your chair and expect yourself to get right back into rhythm with the Divine. All you have to do is stand up. Just stand up and stay there for as long as you need to. Then listen for the music and hear the rhythm and feel the beat. Then, wait for a song to come on that you really love. Then start to move your body to that song you love. Then look up, open your heart, relax your body and let the Divine know you're ready to dance.

What else does it feel like when you're not dancing with the Divine? You may feel insecure, worried or unsure of yourself. Your mind might be racing around constantly, telling you stories that are mostly untrue about why you should stay in this worried place. You may find yourself asking friends and family members constantly to help you make decisions in life as your intuition and sense of trusting your gut has somehow disappeared. Again, these feelings or experiences are a good thing to a certain degree. They are like your internal alarm or warning sign, letting you know that you are off rhythm or that you and the Divine are off in your timing. At this point, you can stop and listen to the music again to get back in rhythm and together in your timing again.

So, how do you know when you are dancing with the Divine? What does it feel like to be guided? Again, everyone experiences this guidance differently, but it will feel like someone or something is whisking you away and carrying you in the right direction and you will know that you're on the right path. It may feel like things are being arranged for you in perfect, synchronistic timing. Life begins to feel like you're flowing with the river or downstream, winding effortlessly around the rocks. Nothing seems to get in your way anymore and, instead, life and opportunities begin to open to you like the parting of the Red Sea. Think of traffic flowing freely on the highway instead of a traffic jam. You may experience a deeper sense of knowing in your heart center that you are being supported by a divinely beautiful, universal energy. You will also come to have complete trust in this Divine energy as you will feel that it only ever has the most loving and kind intentions for you. You will come to understand that you are being shown the way to the people, places, and things that are in your highest good for your soul's growth and development.

The emotions that are most often correlated to the experience of dancing with the Divine include a wide range of positive emotions such as joy, love, gratitude, serenity, hope and a state of being in total awe. And when you become able to sustain a state of being in flow on a more regular basis it is possible to transcend to states of total ecstasy, sheer bliss and being in complete harmony with the universe. Laughter and amusement are also commonplace as you experience some sort of Divine intervention. When you're dancing with the Divine you can expect for things to be arranged for you and to virtually collide with the right people at just the right time. And when your eyes meet with that person that's crossed your path at just the right moment, you will see the essence of the Divine deep within their eyes. When you've asked for something to be brought into your life, felt the gratitude as if it was already in your life, you will experience pure delight as it unfolds in front of you in a better way than you could have possibly imagined. Furthermore, when in flow with the Divine, there is a sense of safety and security that is felt, along with a knowing that you are infinitely supported. When in flow with the Divine, there is an underlying current of grace and ease which lets you know deep inside that you can simply trust the process of life as it unfolds, one moment at a time. You come to a place of understanding that it's more peaceful and magical to simply let go and let the Divine lead you instead of forcing or trying to do things yourself. It will feel like you and the

Divine are moving as one, together with the rhythm of the music and the pulse of the universe. And from the outside, as others observe you, it will look like you're dancing the most beautiful waltz or foxtrot or tango, with the Divine as your partner, leading gracefully on the dance floor of life.

You may or may not even realize that you've experienced this place of being in flow before. Think of the last time that you lost track of time because you were so immersed in the moment. Perhaps you were doing something creative or artistic and didn't notice that you've been there for hours until you stopped and looked up at the clock. Part of you could probably feel that there was indescribable creative energy flowing through you. You were not thinking or analyzing any situation, you were just enjoying being in creative flow. Now, think of the last time you were in nature, a time when you stopped to watch a sunrise or sunset, or a time that you enjoyed being next to a magnificent waterfall. Remember how you were simply in a state of awe and appreciation with how amazing nature can truly be and how powerful yet gentle it can be. Perhaps you could feel the transformative power of the waterfall or you could feel the gentleness of one petal opening at a time on a flower. And in that moment, you could feel how nature is always in flow and consistently unfolding, just as it needs to, in an effortless way.

Dancing with the Divine can also feel like moving to your favorite song or dancing in your living room like no one is watching. Do you know how you do that? With your eyes closed and without any sense of inhibition or being self-conscious. You just turn up the hottest song of the summer and jump or dance around with total freedom, expressing what you feel inside. And if you never do that because you believe you have no rhythm or two left feet, think about the time when you were a kid and you spun around in circles in your front yard, then landed on the grass, giggling in a state of joy, staring at the sky, which looked like it was still spinning and feeling like the ground beneath you was still moving. Remember the bliss and enjoyment of that moment. Not a care in the world. No thoughts or concerns. You were just in a state of being and allowing the laughter to flow through you. This is what it feels like when the Divine moves through you.

Now, imagine for a moment two people dancing the waltz or the salsa on a beautiful wooden dance floor. One-person dancing is obviously the instructor as you can tell by observing the boldness of their arms in dance frame and the succinctness with which they move their feet. The other person dancing is obviously the student as you notice the relaxed shape in their arms as they hold their dance frame and the attempt to move their feet to the rhythm of the music. The instructor is leading the student and guiding them through the movements and the steps, in rhythm and in time with the music. The instructor is strong and confident and clear in their indications of where the student needs to move next, from moment to moment. The student, as they relax and let go, coincides and energetically merges with the instructor. Once trust is established between a leader and a follower, and the two merge into one, the follower can follow, and the leader can lead. Even if the follower doesn't know all the proper steps yet, the leader can guide them gracefully around the room as their dance frame holds them up with pride and supports them. Relaxing and trusting the leader is often the most difficult part for the follower, but letting go is the most essential act for the dance to unfold naturally and for the music to move through both as one entity. The music moves them as they move to the music. The trained eye can see how the dancers express each beat of the music, turning at a very specific part of the song or a dip at just the right time, literally transforming music into movement.

This is exactly what it will feel like when you're dancing with the Divine on the dance floor of life. The scariest part is letting go and allowing the Divine to lead you as you develop that trust, but once you do, the connection is like nothing else in this world and the cooperation is a magnificent experience. The Divine can and will support you every step of the way but only if you get out of your own way. What happens sometimes on the dance floor, when the follower resists the leader in some way, is that toes can get stepped on, stumbling occurs, tension builds, the rhythm is lost, and each partner starts to move on their own instead of in unison. This happens to us in life when we are resisting the support of Divine guidance and trying to do things on our own. It's totally possible to live life this way but somehow it often feels like we're moving against a greater force and it's a lot of hard work. Now, back to the dance floor.

When the dance falls apart because there's a disconnection between the leader and the follower, the leader generally will stop for a moment, invite the follower to relax into the support of their arms and allow their awareness to rest on feeling and sensing the lead. Once the follower surrenders to this and they both tune into the timing and rhythm of the music, they begin to move again in unison with grace and effortless ease. The same applies to your life and moving with the Divine. When you're not in rhythm, you will know it and feel it. Once you take the time to quiet your mind and connect with the Divine again, you will slip back into being in flow together, allowing for things to unfold in their own way and in their own time. You will feel that you're back in rhythm again and pulsing together as one. You will feel that you want to have this dance with the Divine for the rest of your life.

Dance is simply one way of understanding how you can move with and feel connected to the Divine. Many analogies have been used to explain and understand the Divine (or God or Universal Energy) because this power is truly indescribable. Unfortunately, we can lose the essence of it simply by trying to use words to describe it, and so analogy allows us to understand something so profound in a more conceptual way. Dance is simply one way of comprehending this process of letting go and allowing the Divine to guide us to become a co-creator of our life. And it only works when we let go.

Now, the Divine is not only gentle and loving but also omniscient. The Divine is always listening to every thought you have and knows everything about you and only longs to fulfill our heart's desires. I had the most blessed, life-changing experience when I asked the Divine to help me with another situation, related to dancing. For four years, I took Ballroom and Latin dance lessons at a dance studio in Niagara, once or twice a week. My heart and soul enjoyed every moment of it. The dance teachers at the studio were interested in Yoga classes and so we traded equally for those four years. I taught a Yoga class every week for the dance teachers at the studio in exchange for dance lessons. It was a beautiful exchange of learning for everyone that provided physical and spiritual growth. Hence, my deep disappointment when the trade agreement abruptly came to an end after the four years due to some changes in ownership at the studio. Feeling a bit lost about what to do next and where to go for dance lessons, I instead decided to ask the Divine for help.

I asked quite specifically. I said, "Dear Divine, I would like to continue to dance. I LOVE Latin dancing and I don't know where to go. Please help me find a place to practice Latin dancing that is the perfect place for me to grow, learn and have fun. If the dance lessons were free or close to free that would be even better! Thank you, thank you, thank you." Nothing happened for about a week. As someone who is sometimes impatient, I decided to ask again (I know. I'm working on it!). "Dear Divine, I know you're really busy and that you probably heard me the first time, but I just wanted to make sure that you know I'm still looking for a place to continue with my Latin dancing. I'm open to attending whatever dance studio or situation that can help me to fulfill my heart's desire to dance. I'm open to your help and guidance. Thank you." About a week later, I got a phone call from a friend on a Friday afternoon at 3 pm, asking me to go to see a Latin band playing that night in a city that was about an hour away from where we lived, and I said, "Absolutely, yes." Intuitively I knew that I was meant to go hear this Latin band play because my heart was opening and my body resonated with joy at the very thought of it.

That night, as soon as I walked into the room and looked around at the crowd of dancers, there was one man that stood out among the rest. It was like he was "highlighted" for me or "glowing" and I was drawn to him like a magnet. My body was almost pulled in his direction. Not long after, he conveniently asked me to dance salsa with him and as we started speaking he asked if I was interested in attending Social Salsa Dancing in Toronto. He explained that there was a church downtown that had been offering social dance sessions for approximately 10 years now and that it was perfect for people that were new to the Salsa dance scene and it was only $5 entry fee. My eyes lit up at the idea of going and my excitement radiated out of every pore of my being. At the same time, I was laughing inside because I could feel how the Divine had arranged this entire evening for me. Especially since my new Toronto friend proceeded to explain to me that he had no plans of really attending this evening except that a friend had called him around 3:30 pm and asked him to go. I explained that I wasn't planning on attending either until my friend had called to invite me at 3 pm. The situation could not have been arranged any more perfectly in my opinion. I also noted that the social event at the church had been going on in Toronto for 10 years and although I could have gone any other time, the idea of doing so was obviously just outside of my awareness. It had simply never occurred to me to seek out such an opportunity as I did not realize it even existed. Hence, the all-knowing Divine intervention required to show me the way.

The following weekend I attended the Social Salsa dance event at the church in Toronto with my new friend and I was like a kid in a candy store, happy as can be, dancing the afternoon away. I proceeded to attend the Salsa Dance Social almost every weekend for the next year. I transitioned from being "Consciously Competent" as a Salsa dancer to being "Unconsciously Competent" and moving effortlessly with grace and ease. Over the course of the year, I was blessed with meeting many new friends, my Latin dance skills grew exponentially, and I even became confident enough to dance with some of the very best Salsa dancers in Toronto and perform in front of 300 people at a Christmas party within 6 months. Expressing gratitude to the Divine for resolving this situation in a way that was perfect for me simply poured out from my heart every time I was on the dance floor. Magical, simply magical! This experience allowed for the unfolding of the analogy of being led by a partner on the dance floor and what it feels like being led by the Divine.

The one requirement to letting go and allowing yourself to be led, whether that's on a dance floor by a partner or being led by the Divine in life, is vulnerability. Exposing your heart when your partner dips you into a backbend on the dance floor and trusting them to support you is truly a vulnerable and yet beautiful experience. And the more you let go into the backbend the more vulnerable you become, and the more the leader can support you. At the same time, exposing your heart to the Divine means you're also willing to be vulnerable. When you become quiet inside and become aware of your heart's deepest desires and you're not sure how to create that experience because every part of your conscious mind tells you that's "not possible", you must take the risk of being vulnerable, trust that the Divine knows the way to co-create that experience in your life and then let go and allow yourself to be led. Close your eyes and fall back into the arms of the Divine and watch the beauty unfold, one moment at a time with your heart's deepest desires exposed for the whole world to see. When you listen to what your heart holds so tightly inside and you begin to unfold that tightness, you come to understand your soul's purpose in this lifetime. The easiest way to allow that desire to manifest in your life is to let go and allow the Divine to support you every step of the way.

So, go get your dance shoes on and let's hit the floor!

CHAPTER 8:

DANCE SHOES REQUIRED - EMOTIONAL FREEDOM TECHNIQUE

You may want to wear some specific dance shoes along this journey of becoming more connected with the Divine. By dance shoes, I mean tools, techniques, approaches, and methods that will assist in facilitating the process of moving from darkness to light. Shoes that will help facilitate the process of shifting from living life in an unconscious way to becoming a conscious co-creator in your life. These "dance shoes" will become the tools you use to get back into flow and connect with the Divine again. There will be days along this journey that you may feel down and disconnected as you begin to practice this art of dance. You will have short periods and possibly even long periods of not feeling like the Divine is supporting you, which is exactly why you will require a method or tool to get you back in the groove! No one becomes a professional ballroom dancer with just one pair of shoes. Typically, a dancer has several different shoes depending on the outfit or performance. And, to become a professional, chances are pretty good that you're going to wear through and need to replace a couple of pairs of shoes. In this case, I will be providing you with a few different techniques that can cleanse the subconscious mind of limiting beliefs and shift the energetic pattern that surrounds you, allowing you to be more fully present in your life and move from unawareness to awareness. The idea is to find a few different techniques that you're drawn to and that work best for you and to keep them in your toolbox for the days when they are required. The first method, Emotional Freedom Technique, is one of the most effective when it comes to shifting beliefs and transforming your conditioned emotional responses to a thought or past event.

Emotional Freedom Technique (E.F.T.)

E.F.T. is a very powerful tool that will allow you to shift the energetic pattern that surrounds you. That same energetic pattern or vibration that is an accumulation of every past event you have experienced and your emotional reaction to that experience. The energetic pattern that surrounds you and is part of who you are is also a reflection of the beliefs that you hold about yourself and the world based on your past experiences. Perhaps you have experienced a pattern in your life over and over which has frustrated you, hurt you or disempowered you. Maybe you've asked yourself "why does this always happen to me?" and you're motivated to create a new healthy pattern in your life. You know at some level that it's possible to change but you're not sure how exactly. The good news is that you have the power to shift, mold, re-shape and change that energetic vibrational pattern within you and around you. After all, it's your vibration!

The most essential part of this process of transformation is the comprehension that we create our reality from the inside out, not the other way around. Once you conceive that there is nothing really "out there" at all in your external reality but a sea of pure vibration and infinite possibility within an interconnected web of a Divine Universe, then you're on your way to becoming a conscious co-creator with the Divine. The interconnected web of vibration that surrounds us is infinite potential, that simply collapses to create our "reality" as we know it every day when we wake up, so that we can remember who we are and the life story that we've experienced up until this point. Otherwise, you would wake up as a completely different person each day, or not recognize yourself when you looked in the mirror first thing in the morning, which would likely feel like your whole reality was falling apart. Hence, the reason that changing the vibrational pattern that surrounds us takes time and practice. We must shift the vibration, and then continue to vibrate that new pattern until the vibration of the interconnected web that surrounds us collapses into that new pattern and reflects back to us a whole new reality that matches that pattern.

Now, given this theory, it makes sense to apply a tool like Emotional Freedom Technique because the approach is an energetic approach, working at the vibrational level. Emotional Freedom Technique or E.F.T. or "tapping" is one of the most effective and efficient tools to change limiting beliefs, release negative emotions, shift your vibrational pattern, and get back in flow with the Divine. As an E.F.T. practitioner and trainer the two most common questions I receive are:

What is tapping or E.F.T.? How exactly does it work?

E.F.T. is essentially a psychological and emotional form of acupressure or acupuncture. By tapping on the acupuncture points close to the surface of the skin, the technique allows us to change our negative emotional response to a thought or memory to become a more neutral or positive response instead. This new emotional response then allows us to vibrate and radiate at a whole new level, to create a new reality. During the application of E.F.T., you would think a thought or think about an event that you have a negative associative emotional response to. For example, you might think a thought that normally makes you feel anxious or you might remember a specific event from your past that brings up a feeling of hurt or anger. As you think that thought or remember that event, you would start tapping on the acupressure points while saying specific phrases, which then balances the energy system in the body, producing a feeling of being calm or relaxed. As you repeat the process, you think the thought and tap the acupressure points to balance the energy system and feel calm. What happens is that the energy system now has a calm and balanced response to that thought, when it used to produce an anxious or angry vibration. You are re-wiring your emotional and energetic response to that thought so the next time you think that thought, you feel calm and relaxed instead of the original negative emotion. All emotions are really vibration at the subtlest level and so we are simply producing a calmer and balanced energetic response to the original thought. What most people find is that the memory stays the same, but they feel differently when they think about it. Or, a new thought or way of viewing the event comes to mind.

Thought or Memory = Negative Emotional Response/Vibration

Thought or Memory + Tapping on Acupressure Points = Feeling Calm and Relaxed

Repeat the Tapping Process and now...

Thought or Memory = Neutral or Positive Emotional Response/Vibration

Continuing to apply E.F.T. then produces a new vibrational pattern and then a new reality can be reflected back to you that is a mirror for that new vibration.

The easiest way to understand how E.F.T. works is to review Pavlov's Dog Experiment in Psychology which demonstrates "classical conditioning" and how stimulus/response happens. In Pavlov's experiment, he would ring a bell every time before he would feed the dogs. Eventually, the dogs would automatically begin to salivate as soon as they heard the bell as they had associated the sound of the bell with being fed. The stimulus was the sound of the bell and the conditioned, automatic response was for the dogs to begin salivating. Your pets, if you have any, probably do the same thing. When they hear the sound of the can of dog or cat food opening and the sound of their bowl hitting the floor, they come running as fast as they can! Now, although it was not part of the experiment, I want you to imagine for a moment that the next time we rang a bell, we led the dogs to the front door to be let outside instead. Initially, the dogs would be confused and probably salivating as they went out the door. But, if we repeated the process, by ringing the bell and letting the dogs outside again and again, eventually the dogs would become conditioned to associate the stimulus of the bell sounding with going to the door to be let outside.

You also have thousands of "conditioned responses" that have been wired in your brain, based on the many experiences you've had in your life. Take a moment to hear the sound of the song from your wedding day, and notice the emotional response in your body. Think about the graduation song and an image from your high school, college or university graduation, and then notice the emotional response in your body. Take a moment, in your mind, to hear the voice of one of your parents nagging you to do something and notice your emotional response. Now, think of an image of a loved one and hear the sound of their voice telling you how much they care about you and appreciate you. Once again, notice your emotional response connected to that. We all have a multitude of complex associative emotional responses to a wide variety of thoughts. These are first established in our formative years and are the basis for the deeper-rooted beliefs that we have about the world and others. The emotions that you feel on the most regular basis every day are what contributes to your energetic body and the reality that is mirrored back to you by consciousness itself. Some of your emotional, conditioned responses may be positive ones that create a beautiful reality for you. However, some of your responses may be negative and therefore impeding you from experiencing a more beautiful reality. E.F.T. works wonders when it comes to re-wiring those emotional responses so that you can, in fact, experience a different reality.

E.F.T. is essentially the tool we would use to feel differently about a situation from the past, present or future. Think of an example of a friend who constantly complains about being hurt or angry in his or her life, even though the initial event happened years ago. Every time they tell that story, they strengthen the neural pathway in the brain of that thought and they also strengthen the emotional response to it. This means they also strengthen that in the vibration around them, making it more likely for them to experience similar situations, so that the same neural pathway that feels "normal" to them can be fired again. They may not like the feeling, especially since they're complaining about it, but it feels normal or comfortable because they feel it on a regular basis and the opposite feeling, perhaps joy or peace, would feel awkward or unfamiliar to them. The good news is that the body and brain can be reconditioned to feel that new feeling on a regular basis and E.F.T. is one of the greatest tools to facilitate that process. We can rewire our most significant negative emotional responses to create more positive emotions. Next, we allow the Divine to take over and guide us to more situations and people in our lives that are more in line with those positive emotions!

E.F.T. can be used to re-wire a wide range of emotions and issues including fear, phobias, anxiety, a craving for substances, anger, sadness, grief, jealousy, insecurity, physical pain, childhood traumas and more. Gary Craig, the original founder of the technique, would say to "try it on everything!" You can apply E.F.T. to any negative belief, any physical discomfort, and any negative emotion that is not serving you. If you're practicing co-creating with the Divine using meditation and mental imagery (as described in previous chapters) to focus on what you do want to create in your life but you only notice the "lack" of that being in your life at the present time, then you can use E.F.T. as a tool to neutralize that feeling of lack. The more you focus on something not being part of your life, when you really want it, the more you can create a feeling of lack. Tapping on the issue can bring you to a place of being at peace in the moment and therefore more easily allow that which you do desire to be birthed, coincidently, from the interconnected web of the Universe.

The other most common question about E.F.T. is how to do it? Usually, it sounds more like, "What? You want me to tap on my face and body, say some things, and then roll my eyes? Are you being serious?", and my response is always "YES!". Although the full description of the process of E.F.T. and all the intricate ways in which it can be most effectively applied is beyond the scope of this book, you will find the

Basics (as initially taught by Gary Craig) below, as well as many professional resources listed at the end of this Chapter.

The Basics of E.F.T. are like the qualities of a great sandwich. You will have the olive on top, which will represent the "Set-Up Statement", the top layer of bread which will represent the first round of "tapping the points", the middle part of the sandwich which will represent the "Gamut Point Procedure", and the bottom layer of bread which will represent another round of "tapping the points".

E.F.T. – The Basics

First, let's look at all the acupressure points on the face and body so that you can familiarize yourself with them. There is a specific sequence used for this tapping process; starting at the top and working your way down as indicated in the image below:

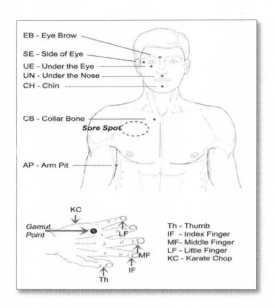

EB - Eye Brow
SE - Side of Eye
UE - Under the Eye
UN - Under the Nose
CH - Chin

CB - Collar Bone
Sore Spot

AP - Arm Pit

KC
Gamut Point
LF
MF
IF
Th

Th - Thumb
IF - Index Finger
MF- Middle Finger
LF - Little Finger
KC - Karate Chop

Step 1:
Choose the Tapping Topic

Take a moment to think of a very specific thought or memory that you would like to re-wire your emotional response to. Tune into the emotion and identify it. Hold the thought or the image in your mind that elicits that emotion, because that is the image that you want to re-wire your response to. The key is to be as specific as possible when choosing a thought or memory. Using E.F.T. to improve self-esteem, for example, is very possible but it's more important to tap on memories of events that have contributed to low self-esteem, instead of tapping on just low self-esteem in general. E.F.T. can shift and transform self-esteem, but tapping on one issue at a time that you know

204

contributed to your low self -esteem, will be most effective to improve self-esteem, as your sub-conscious will no longer be operating from that place. Once you have the thought, memory or image in mind that you want to re-wire your emotional response to, measure the intensity of the emotion on a "Discomfort Scale" of 1 to 10, with "10" being intense discomfort of the negative emotion and "1" being calm and neutral. Remember your number!

Step 2:
Develop the Set-Up Statement and Reminder Phrase

The next step will represent the olive on the top part of the sandwich. We will develop a Set-Up Phrase that you can use before you begin the round of tapping the points. We start with the Set-Up Phrase so that there can be an acknowledgment of the problem and acceptance of the self. The Set-Up is specific and accurately describes the problem. The phrase is a way of stating that you want to shift from feeling this negative emotion to feel that you love and accept yourself, regardless of the problem. The standard Set-Up phrase is:

"Even though I have this _problem_, I deeply and completely love and accept myself"

When the Set-Up Phrase is said out loud you will replace the word "problem" with the negative emotion that you feel when you think the thought that you identified in Step 1. Perhaps the thought makes you feel anxious, worried, angry, sad, frustrated, confused, or disappointed. Whatever it is, you can simply say the word instead of saying "problem". You can also elaborate or change this set-up phrase to be even more specific to the issue you're working on. Some different examples include:

Even though I have this <u>negative emotion</u>, maybe I can choose to see the situation differently.

Even though I have this <u>negative emotion</u>, I wonder if I can open up my mind and feel love and compassion instead.

Even though I have this <u>negative emotion</u>, perhaps I can choose to tell the story a different way.

And here are some more specific examples of how to construct the Set-Up statement in order to shift from how we are currently feeling to how we would like to feel instead:

Even though I have this <u>anger</u> about that fight with my sister, I wonder if I could choose to forgive her instead and see her point of view.

Even though I have this <u>anxiety</u> about the deadline at work, maybe I could choose to feel calm and relaxed instead.

Even though I have this <u>disappointed feeling</u> about my relationship, I invite my heart to feel differently about what happened.

Even though I feel <u>disconnected</u> from the Divine right now, I allow myself to relax, get back in flow and trust Divine guidance.

Keep in mind that there are infinite ways to construct the Set-Up statement and no wrong way of doing it. Allow yourself to become more creative with it once you have a better understanding of the technique and how it works. However, when you are just getting started with the technique it can be best to keep it simple and use the first example which is a very effective general statement.

Now, as you move down the body, tapping the different points you will say a **Reminder Phrase.** The Reminder Phrase is designed to keep the mind's attention on the issue that you are re-wiring your associative response to. The phrase is simply repeating the "problem", which is the emotion or the feeling that you decided on in Step 1. You can simply repeat:

"This _problem_"

Instead of saying the word "problem" though, you can say the negative emotion you experience when you think about the event or situation. So, it would instead be this "anger" or this "anxiety" or this "disappointed feeling", for example. Many people ask why they would want to continue to focus on the problem, as opposed to the solution, which is a valid question. The reason is that once you fire the neural pathway, or thought pattern connected to the negative emotion, the relaxing effect of the tapping can then rewire the associative response to that thought. This means that the next time you have that thought you will feel relaxed instead of the negative emotion, and what most people find is that their thoughts about the event or situation automatically change. As a result, they experience a more positive emotion instead, without trying to force it in any way.

Step 3:
Getting Started!

Begin by saying the Set-Up phrase that you developed, out loud, 3 times while rubbing the Sore Spot (lymphatic drainage point) or tapping the Karate Chop point on the side of the hand. See the diagram above for the locations. The lymphatic drainage point helps rid the body of toxins, waste and other unwanted materials. When you press and rub it in a circle, you are helping your body disperse any congestion there. Alternatively, you can tap the Karate Chop point on the side of the hand or tap both karate chop points together. Saying the Set-Up statement out loud with emphasis, from your heart, can allow the process to be more effective as well.

Step 4:

Tapping the Points

This next part will represent the bread on the top part of the sandwich. Repeat the "Reminder phrase" that you developed, while tapping on each of the following acupressure points approximately 7 times:

Inner part of the Eye Brow (EB), Side of the Eye (SE), Under the Eye (UE), Under the Nose (UN), Chin Point (CH), Collarbone point (CB), Under the arm (UA), Thumb (TH), Index Finger (IF), Middle Finger (MF), Baby Finger (BF), Karate Chop Point (KC)

You can use your index finger and middle fingers together to tap all the points. You can tap either down the right side of the body or left side or you can alternate sides. It is your choice. Keep in mind you can also tap using both hands for the eyebrow point, side of the eyes, under the eyes, collarbone points and under the arms. You can also tap the finger points on the right hand or the left hand. Tap with enough strength that you can feel it but that you're also not hurting yourself in the process. Each tapping point is connected to a different Chinese energy meridian line and it's best to tap each point in the sequence. However, if you miss a tapping point there is no cause for concern and you will likely still feel relief and the changes from tapping.

Step 5:

Eye Movements

This next part will represent the middle part of the sandwich. This part is known as the **Gamut Point Procedure** and is seemingly strange at first until you understand the purpose and importance behind it. While tapping the Gamut point on the back of the hand (see diagram) you will perform a sequence of eye moments. If you prefer you can also just press and hold the Gamut point instead of tapping. The eye movements are specifically designed to help the brain relax and allow for the processing of any past events connected to intense emotions. What is happening is something called "bilateral stimulation of the brain". For example, when your eyes look to the right you are firing the left hemisphere of the brain and when your eyes look to the left, it is firing the right hemisphere. This repeated stimulation of both sides of the brain creates a "whole brain" experience or a blending of both hemispheres. This blending of both hemispheres of the brain has also been used in other well-known forms of trauma therapy techniques including Eye Movement Desensitization and Reprocessing (EMDR). It is also similar to Rapid Eye Movement or REM sleep which is the dream state of sleep. Dreams are the result of our brains trying to segregate, analyze and file away the data that we have absorbed during the day. And so, the eye movements of the Gamut Point Procedure, EMDR, and REM sleep all allow for the brain to synthesize and process emotions and past experiences, fully and completely. The Gamut Point Procedure has the potential to assist the brain in processing stored emotions related to different events, both big and small.

For the Gamut Point Procedure, you will tap or hold the Gamut Point and then, without moving your head:

Look down hard to the right

Look down hard to the left

Roll your eyes in a circle

Roll your eyes the other way

Look horizontal left and horizontal right approximately 5 times

At this time, you will likely feel a shift in your emotions, naturally, take a deep breath in and out, or experience a calmer and relaxed feeling. Although it is very rare if you experience a headache at all from the eye movements you can skip the Gamut point procedure.

Step 6:

More Tapping

This next part will represent the bread on the bottom part of the sandwich. Repeat the tapping sequence and continue to say the "Reminder phrase" that you developed while going back up and tapping on each of the following acupressure points approximately 7 times:

Inner part of the Eye Brow (EB), Side of the Eye (SE), Under the Eye (UE), Under the Nose (UN), Chin Point (CH), Collarbone point (CB), Under the arm (UA),

Thumb (TH), Index Finger (IF), Middle Finger (MF), Baby Finger (BF), Karate Chop Point (KC)

Sometimes, you may want to add in another tapping point which is at the top of the head or the crown of the head. This point is also known as the Crown Chakra in yoga and is also where many of the Chinese energy meridian points meet. This is the time to reinstall the positive part at the end of your Setup statements. So, as you tap the crown of your head you would say:

I love and accept myself anyway.

I choose now to see the situation through the eyes of love and compassion.

I choose now to be in flow with the Divine Universe.

I allow myself to forgive and let go.

I choose now to tell the story a different way.

Or…any other positive affirmation that takes you to a state or emotion that is the opposite of the negative emotion that you started tapping on. This is a nice way to finish any round of tapping.

Step 7:
Stop and Assess

Now, stop, take a deep breath and let go. You've just completed one round of tapping on one specific issue. Go back and think of the image, the event, the situation or the thought that you originally started with before tapping. Sense how you feel when you think about it now. Assess your intensity level of discomfort of emotion (Subjective Units of Discomfort or SUDS) and compare it to the original level of discomfort. If your number is now a 0 that's great and you can move onto to a whole different issue. If your number has increased (which is unlikely) you may need to become more specific with the issue you're tapping on. The majority of the time you will find that your number on the discomfort scale has decreased or that you're now able to feel more relaxed or differently when you think of the situation or event. Some people describe the emotion as feeling more "distant" or the scene feels more "far away" in their mind. If you're not quite at a 0 yet on that scale of 1 to 10, it is important to continue tapping to clear the issue completely so that there is no emotional reaction or that you feel differently about it. You can repeat for a few more rounds if necessary.

Step 8:

Another Round of Tapping

This part will represent going back up to the top part of the sandwich and starting over. Simply repeat Steps 3, 4, 5 and 6 with adjustments as follows:

- ❖ Substitute the Set-Up Phrase you used with: "Even though I **still** have some of this emotion, I deeply and completely accept myself". Or whatever Set up statement you started with. We simply want to

> acknowledge that there is still some of the same issue that we are tapping on.

❖ And the substitute the Reminder Phrase then becomes: "This **remaining** emotion". The idea is to continue tapping until the emotion no longer remains.

Once you've done Steps 3 to 6 again, stop and assess again, which is Step 7. If you need to do another round of tapping, do as many as you need to until the issue is cleared. There is no limit to how much tapping you can do, and there is no harm that can be done. You will know when you're done tapping on a particular issue or thought because you will literally feel differently about it. Your experience may be that it wouldn't make sense to feel the original way you did about the situation or that because the original feeling doesn't "match" anymore, you are able to think differently about it. Some people are even able to laugh at the situation and that's one way of knowing you've cleared it completely with E.F.T. because that is true freedom!

Important E.F.T. Tips

Most people who are new to E.F.T. and tapping attempt to tap on an issue that is too large and diverse to tackle all at once. The importance of breaking down an issue and identifying all the different aspects is essential for E.F.T. to really provide the optimal healing benefits. Let's look at the example of tapping on 'fear of spiders' for example. For someone who has a significant fear or true phobia, simple tapping on "this fear of spiders" may only provide minimal relief. However, if we broke that issue down into the different "aspects" you would likely discover that there is a fear of the spider biting, an aversion to the way it moves, a fear of touching or being touched by the spider, an aversion to the way their legs move or a fear of their fuzzy bodies. Each of these issues would need to be tapped on during separate rounds until they each are a zero on a discomfort scale. This process of identifying all the different "aspects" related to a fear requires some deeper insight into the issue and being as specific as you can.

Another example of identifying all aspects related to an issue would be tapping on emotions and memories related to a car accident. If you simply apply E.F.T. to "this accident" it is likely too diverse to feel significant changes, however, if you identify the aspects first and tap on them separately you will experience relief. Some "aspects" may include: remembering the brake lights of the car in front, the feeling of pressing the break but not slowing down fast enough, the sight of the guardrail approaching quickly, the feeling of not having any control, sounds in the car of someone screaming and the actual impact itself. Each of these aspects would need to be approached delicately and one at a time until they are individually cleared. Keep in mind that processing a significant traumatic event is best done with a qualified practitioner.

You may also need to examine how events in your childhood contributed to a pattern you are currently experiencing in your adult life. If you are using E.F.T. to change a belief system, such as not feeling worthy or deserving of love, you need to tap on the events in adulthood and childhood that contributed to that belief system of not feeling deserving of love, as opposed to just trying to tap on "not feeling worthy". Tapping on a complex, deeply rooted belief can take time and insight. Think of it more like a "not worthy" forest of trees. Each tree represents an event in your life that contributed to not feeling worthy. Perhaps one tree represents that time when your parents forgot to pick you up from school, and another tree represents a time when a teacher told you that you didn't deserve to pass a grade, and yet another tree is the time when you were rejected by a girl that you asked out. Each of the "trees" or events need to be tapped on one at a time so that the "not worthy" forest disappears entirely. So, if you're aware of the belief system you desire to change and transform, take the time to write down all the events that may have contributed to that belief in your lifetime, and begin to tap on them one at a time. You don't necessarily have to tap on each event that ever happened in your life but start with the significant ones that you know are where the belief started. You will know that the belief has eventually shifted when your life starts to shift and change too. The external reality, the mirror, your world, will begin to reflect to you your new level of worthiness that you start to feel.

E.F.T. can truly be a beautiful and magical way to reshape our reality from the inside out. As you begin to shift and change the energy and vibration that surrounds you and allow yourself to remain in flow with the Divine, your life will begin to change. The changing of reality only happens from the inside out, not the other way around. Whether you use E.F.T. to clear a simple concern or worry in your life, to change a deeper held belief system or to process significant trauma in your life, you will inevitably feel more connected to the Divinity that is already within you and supporting you in this life. The interconnected web of this Divine Universe will shift and change and open doors for you simply because you've changed, and your energy has changed.

Again, a deeper understanding of E.F.T., all the ways it can be applied, and its infinite healing properties are beyond the scope of this book. However, there is a significant amount of information that can be found online about E.F.T. and the most reliable and professional sources include:

www.eftdvds.com

www.emofree.com

www.eftuniverse.com

www.thetappingsolution.com

CHAPTER 9:

OTHER DANCE SHOES REQUIRED – YOGA AND MEDITATION

More than just one pair of dance shoes will be required for this long journey of evolving awareness and connecting at a deeper and deeper level with the Divine. In addition to using E.F.T., practicing yoga and meditation are also powerful methods that allow us to clear energetic blockages in order to increase our awareness and develop a relationship with the Divine essence within us. The practice of yoga and meditation can assist in learning how to quiet the mind so that you can receive that guidance from Divine Source energy. When the mind is busy and focused externally, it is much more difficult to let yourself be led by your heart, your intuition or Divine messages. It's easy to miss synchronistic events when the mind is busy, focused on other things. The practice of yoga allows us to come back to the present moment and connect with the physical body. The actual definition of the word "yoga" literally means "unity" or "to yoke," or the union of body and mind. The practice of yoga typically includes physical and mental disciplines for attaining liberation from the material world and union of the self with the Divine. In yoga, the physical postures, breathing exercises, meditation, and relaxation are used to achieve control of the body and mind and experience tranquility. Most importantly, the practice allows us to unite ourselves with the Divine through the stillness of the mind. There is a more detailed explanation of yoga found in the Yoga Sutras, the ancient philosophical text written by Patanjali. The second sutra states: "yoga chitta vritti nirodha", which is understood to be translated as "Yoga is the restriction of the fluctuations of consciousness" (translation by George Feuerstein). Another way of understanding this is that yoga is the cessation of the fluctuations of the mind or the quieting of the mind. Therefore, the practice of yoga can allow one to achieve stillness and clarity of mind. It is then and only then that the individual can experience their true nature which is wholeness and absolute Divinity.

So, if you always thought yoga was just about doing downward dog and headstands in a hot room, it's essential to know that there is much more depth to the practice. Yoga is a consistent way of revealing more of your Divine nature to yourself. It is regular work and effort to strengthen a new healthy pattern of movement in your body, and a method to find the quiet place in between thoughts so that you can hear Divine guidance to get out of your own way and live the life your soul came here to experience. The physical practice of yoga, also known as asana, is very important but maybe not for the reason you believe it to be.

"You cannot do yoga. Yoga is your natural state. What you can do are yoga exercises, which may reveal to you where you are resisting your natural state." ~Sharon Gannon~

Yoga "exercises", or asanas, are the physical practice that most people in North America have come to understand as the practice of yoga. Although the practice of yoga varies depending on the style, most practices include asanas (physical postures), pranayama (breath work), meditation, relaxation and some form of spiritual development. The physical asanas or exercises are better understood to be the vehicle through which we achieve the state of yoga or our natural state, which is the ultimate connection with Divine source energy. During your physical practice of yoga, you will have the delight of becoming aware of where you are "resisting" this natural state.

How will you come to know where you are resisting this natural state? If you already practice yoga, think about the poses that you love to do the most. Perhaps you really love arm balancing poses, or you really enjoy standing balancing poses. Ask yourself what you enjoy most about them. Perhaps they are easy for you or you can feel a sense of achievement when you're in them. However, these are not necessarily the poses you need to be practicing most often. Take a moment to think about the poses that you avoid as much as possible. Perhaps you avoid back bending poses because you find them difficult or maybe you avoid forward bending poses because you have always had tight hamstrings and trouble letting go. These are the poses which reveal to you where you are resisting your natural state. And if you have never practiced yoga before, simply be open to the experience and notice your internal response to each posture. To a trained eye, the energetic, emotional and physical blockages can often be seen when observing someone in a yoga posture. Whether that is tightness in the hips and low back or trouble opening the heart in a back-bending posture. Typically, the physical blockages in a yoga posture, at the deepest of vibrational levels, can be representative of blockages that person is experiencing in their life off the yoga mat. And so, how does one work through such blocks? Simply by practicing the poses that you prefer not to do. To face and work through the physical blocks is ideal. Assuming there is no medical reason for you to avoid them, practicing the poses where you experience the most resistance will eventually lead to more freedom in that pose. You can only work through any block, whether that's in a yoga asana or in your life in general, by facing it, staring it straight in the eye, and loving yourself enough to stay present with it until it fades into pure awareness.

> *"There is a way through every block."* ~
> *Yogi Bhajan* ~

The good news is that there is always a way to move through blocks in yoga postures and in your life. Although they may seem separate at first, with consistent yoga practice, you will likely become aware of the connection between blocks in certain asanas and blocks in your life, such as a blocked heart or trouble letting go and being in flow. The blocks that you experience in a yoga posture, such as tight shoulders or locked up hips, can be connected as well to stored emotions that are held tightly in the body at a vibrational level. As we open the physical body in asanas, we can release those stored emotions. This allows for the vibrational energy around the body to shift and change. As a result, your life changes as well since the external world you experience must vibrate back to you differently as you begin to vibrate at a different frequency. This is the same reason why E.F.T. can help you to move through emotional blocks in your life. The physical postures in yoga can assist you to move through the same blocks with a different approach. Since the body and mind are not separate, but rather intricately connected, you can approach the block via the mind with E.F.T. or via the body with asanas. Either way, you move through the block and become better able to connect with the Divine in the process. However, only focusing on the physical aspect and asanas in a yoga practice is akin to going to a delicious buffet and only having a salad. In addition to physical postures, in yoga practice, there is also meditation which is a vital component.

When most people think of meditation, they think of an image of someone sitting peacefully and effortlessly in a cross-legged position, somewhere in nature or on a yoga mat. And although meditation can allow us to achieve a blissful, stillness in our minds, it does take practice, practice and more practice for most people to reach that state of bliss and feel connected with the Divine. Take a moment to go back to the art of practicing and the "vinyl record" principle in Chapter 5. When you first begin a meditation practice it can be frustrating because there is no "groove in the record" or neural pathway in the brain yet that leads to that still quiet place in the mind. What happens initially is that the mind races around, thinking incessantly about unnecessary and irrelevant thoughts. And then, one day, in your practice, you experience a moment of blissful, quiet stillness because the thinking stopped. Not by effort or by wrestling with the mind, but rather by simply moving into the observant mind and noticing the present moment. And when you've done it once, you can do it again. Not by trying but by allowing. And you deepen the "groove in the record" that allows you to achieve that quiet, blissful state. This means that it eventually becomes easier to access that state and you can stay there for longer and longer durations. Another way of understanding the process of meditation is to review the four stages that one goes through when learning anything new.

Before you begin to meditate, you are probably unaware that you don't know how to meditate. You may not recognize the benefits of meditating, or you're not interested in learning how to meditate as you've been going through life just fine without it. The next stage is when you come to realize that it would be beneficial to practice meditation because you've heard it does wonders for mental and physical health and you become aware of the fact that you have difficulty quieting your own mind. The next stage is when you begin to practice meditation and suddenly become aware of just how much your mind races as you begin to notice and observe your thoughts. You experience moments of bliss when you can quiet the mind, however, they are brief and require a great deal of focus. The last stage is when you're able to move into that relaxed brain wave state of meditation within a matter of minutes and stay for longer and longer durations because you've been practicing how to get there daily. You may even feel a sense of connectedness and oneness with all that is or a sense of being connected to something much greater than yourself. With daily practice, this can be achieved but the key, of course, is practice and finding the right type of meditation that fits with you and your lifestyle. The more you can practice, like anything, the easier it gets.

> *"You should sit in meditation for twenty minutes every day — unless you're too busy. Then you should sit for an hour." ~*
> *Zen proverb~*

The biggest reason most people don't meditate, even if they know it could possibly have life-changing potential, is because they believe that they don't have the time. And the busier we are, the less we feel like we have time to meditate. However, the paradox is, the busier we are, the more likely it is that our mind is racing and needs meditation more than it needs to accomplish something else on the "To-Do List". The busier the mind gets, the busier the mind gets. And the better you get at filling every moment of your day, the better you get at adding more things to fill your tomorrow. And you find yourself, waiting, wanting and wishing for just a moment of peace! The irony is you can experience that moment of peace that you desire in any passing moment. You can become conscious of the moment at any time, simply by being fully present. You can observe and experience the world without any filter of the thinking, analytical mind. In such a moment, you will be able to see the Divine essence that is within you and within all living things around you. To begin living this way does require that you take some time out of your busy life to practice meditation so that you can create that "groove in the record" or neural pathways in your brain. Once you do, you will have access to that state of mind at other times during the day, not necessarily when you're sitting in a chair or on a yoga mat to practice. Whether it's meditating for two minutes, ten minutes, twenty minutes or an hour a day, know that you are deepening that groove in the record, more and more each time you sit to practice.

So what type of meditation is right for you? There are many different types of meditation and it is important to find the one that is right for you. Some types of meditation that you may be familiar with include Mindfulness (Vipassana) Meditation, Transcendental Meditation, Holosync, Zen or Guided Visualization. Mantra can also be used as a form of meditation which is often a beneficial practice for beginners as it gives them something specific to focus on. Silent meditation or just observing the present moment can be difficult for beginners as the mind has difficulty settling. Mantra meditation gives the mind something to settle upon. Mantra literally translates as an "instrument of the mind" or a tool that you can use to enter a state of meditation. This tool is often an ancient powerful sound or vibration that can change the energy that surrounds you as you chant out loud or repeat it in your mind. It changes the essence of who you are because you're focusing your attention on the vibration of words that represent the Divine essence. As you begin to chant and meditate on the sounds of the Divine, you begin to vibrate with the Divine, making it that much easier for your life to be in flow and easily move through perceived blocks.

"Vibrate the cosmos, and the cosmos shall clear the path." ~ Yogi Bhajan ~

Words and mantras have power as they have a vibrational frequency to them. This means that as you repeat these mantras, you are tapping into the 84 energy meridian lines that are connected at the palate at the roof of the mouth and as a result, you are shifting your energetic pattern. Everything in the Universe has a vibratory frequency to it, including you and your life. By chanting ancient Kundalini mantras, you are vibrating a combination of sounds and tuning into different levels of consciousness and power. We are creating our reality with every word we speak and every thought we think. Some of the possible benefits of chanting mantra include having prosperity, peace of mind, increasing intuition and overcoming obstacles. By simply chanting them, we are vibrating at a different level which then has an effect on our lives. There are some specific mantras in the Kundalini tradition that can be very helpful to meditate on to become more connected with your intuitive guidance system and the Divine. Each mantra has a very specific vibration and purpose which means that you can use the most appropriate mantra for whatever challenge you are experiencing or whatever desired outcome you have.

Some specific examples are listed below and are written in the Gurmukhi language. For more information or to listen to the mantras you can go to www.spiritvoyage.com.

1) **Adi Mantra** – Ong Namo Guru Dev Namo

This mantra is chanted 3 times at the beginning of every Kundalini class and is a method of "tuning in" and calling upon the creative consciousness or the Divine. Typically, it is recommended to chant this mantra before other mantras so that you are first connected to a higher consciousness. The literal translation of the mantra is: I bow to the Creator. I bow to the Divine Teacher. **Ong** means the Creator, **Namo** means to call upon, or to greet, **Guru** is the Teacher or the force that brings one from darkness into light. **Dev** means transparent or unbounded light. Yogi Bhajan, the author of the mantra, states to "Use this mantra in its complete form anytime you have a lack of faith. With the grace of Guru Ram Das, when this mantra is chanted, the total spiritual knowledge of all teachers who have ever existed or who will ever exist on this Earth is in that person." This mantra essentially links you to the "Golden Chain" of teachers who brought Kundalini yoga to the world.

2) **Magic Manta** - Ek Ong Kar Sat Gur Prasad, Sat Gur Prasad Ek Ong Kar

This mantra is known as the "magic mantra" due to its ability to transform a negative situation into a positive situation. The author of the mantra is Guru Nanak Dev Ji. The mantra literally means: "There is one Creator of all Creation. All is a blessing of the One Creator. This realization comes through Guru's Grace." After chanting it, it is wise to keep your thoughts and words positive, as you will be in a state of manifestation. The mantra takes a negative thought and reverses it to come out positive. A thought rides into your consciousness to be processed with "Ek Ong Kar Sat Gur Prasad," and comes out pure with, "Sat Gur Prasad Ek Ong Kar." It is recommended that you chant this mantra with reverence and respect due to its powerful, transformative capabilities.

3) **Mantra for Universal Consciousness**: Ang Sang Wahe Guru

This mantra is one that recognizes the universal consciousness within each of us. The author of this mantra is Guru Amar Das. It literally translates as: "The dynamic, living ecstasy of the universe is dancing within every cell of me". The dynamic, loving energy of the Infinite Source of All is dancing within my every cell and is present in my every limb. My individual consciousness merges with the Universal Consciousness.

According to Gurucharan Singh, the Kundalini Research Institute Director of Training;

Ang is 'a part'. Sang is 'in every,' or 'with every'. Wahe is 'the indescribable living ecstasy of Infinite Being'. Guru is 'the knowledge that transforms your mind, emotion, and essence.' The whole phrase means, "The Infinite Being, God, is with me, and vibrates in every molecule and cell of my being." This mantra expresses a universal truth. Repeating it creates a thought, which gradually guides the psyche to adjust itself. It re-connects every fragmented projection of the psyche, each separated part of the body, and synchronizes the finite sense of self to the Infinite Oneness. This act of rejoining the separated parts is the quintessential act of healing. Under attack, under war, under the pressures of fear, this meditation keeps us together, conscious and ready to act. It brings the inner peacefulness that comes only from the touch and scope of spirit.

4) **Mantra to Move through Difficult Situations** – Guru Gaitri Mantra

The author of this powerful and beautiful mantra is Guru Gobind Singh. The mantra is: Gobinday, Mukunday, Udaaray, Apaaray, Hariang, Kariang, Nirnamay, Akamay. And each of the words translated consecutively means Sustainer, Liberator, Enlightener, Infinite, Destroyer, Creator, Nameless and Desireless. This is a wonderful mantra that has the power to assist in the process to let go of fear, attachment, and pain. After chanting continuously, situations seem to work out magically and the future becomes smoother! It works more effectively if you chant repeatedly and you can do so out loud or in your mind. The best time to chant can be when you are in the midst of an emotional challenge, crisis or feeling like there's no way out of a situation. The challenge is to not be consumed by the situation but rather to focus on the mantra and let it do the work. Let the mantra assist you in overcoming the worry, fear, sadness or frustration. When your vibration changes, things outside of you shift miraculously in a very natural and beautiful way. The mantra is powerful in the sense that it can help you to break through deep-seated blocks and beliefs. "Besides helping cleanse the subconscious mind, it balances the hemispheres of the brain, bringing compassion and patience to the one who meditates on it." - Yogi Bhajan

5) **Mantra for Healing** – Ra Ma Da Sa, Sa Say So Hung

The author of this soft and lovely mantra is Yogi Bhajan himself. The translation of the mantra is:

Ra - Sun

Ma - Moon

Da - Earth

Sa - Impersonal Infinity

Sa Say - Totality of Infinity

So - Personal sense of merger and identity

Hung - The infinite, vibrating and real.

This mantra is known as the ultimate healing tool as it connects one with the beautiful energies of the sun, moon, earth and the Infinite Spirit to bring deep healing. It can be chanted to heal the self or to send healing energy to anyone you wish. The mantra heals by tuning the soul's vibration to the vibration of the Universe, which is completely pure and without physical or emotional pain. This mantra also stimulates the flow of Kundalini energy within the central channel of the spine to assist in healing the body. This flow of new energy can bring us back into energetic balance. This mantra seems to capture the healing light of the Universe and then with our intention we can direct it out to ourselves, others or the entire planet.

Of course, mantras are simply one type of meditation that many people find effective and helpful, especially if you have a difficult time allowing the mind to settle and relax because the mantra can give the mind something to focus on. At the same time, if you do not feel drawn to mantras then it is important to find a type of meditation that is right for you. The first question you may want to ask yourself is why you want to learn to meditate or what purpose it might serve for you. If you are a beginner when it comes to meditation and you're interested in listening to unique sounds that can help your mind to slow down, then you may want to explore a type of meditation called Holosync or Binaural Beats. Holosync develops new neural pathways, creates a whole brain experience and allows you to experience a theta or delta brain wave state. You can find more information at www.centerpointe.com. For a more advanced 3 dimensional version of Binaural Beats meditation, that has a Gamma wave embedded in the background and can assist in developing your intuition, you can check out http://bit.ly/SynctuitionCCC. If you are interested in a disciplined practice that allows for self-transformation through self-observation than you may consider attending a Vipassana meditation retreat center. Since the time of Buddha, Vipassana has been passed down through an unbroken chain of teachers and the practice is designed to teach one to maintain equanimity of the mind in order to be at peace and experience true happiness. You can find out more at www.dhamma.org. Furthermore, if your reason for learning to meditate is to begin to raise your level of energy, merge with the quantum field and begin to consciously co-create your reality with the Divine you may want to explore mental imagery or visualization. You can also use powerful emotions in mental imagery to begin to change your life. For more information on this process, you can go to www.drjoedispenza.com.

In addition to asana and meditation, pranayama is also a vital component of the potential life-changing transformation that can happen with the practice of yoga. Pranayama is also referred to as "breath control" or "mastering the life force energy" since the breath is what sustains life every waking moment. By learning to manage the breath we can learn to manage our internal state, our nervous system and our levels of energy. Following the breath is one of the best ways to anchor us into the present moment as it is always with us regardless of what's happening for us in the day. The quality of the breath can also be a clear indicator of our internal state. For example, the breath will become short, rapid and shallow when we are stressed, and the sympathetic nervous system is being stimulated. At the same time, when the parasympathetic nervous system is engaged, and we are feeling relaxed, the breath becomes long, deep and slow. Again, yoga is the practice of observing and changing our internal state instead of consistently trying to control something outside of ourselves. This means that even if we are in a stressful situation and the sympathetic nervous system is stimulated, triggering the breath to shorten, we then can recognize what's happening on the inside and begin to lengthen the breath. As we do so, we are choosing to engage the relaxation response or parasympathetic nervous system. As we move into Dirga Pranayama or Three-Part Complete breath, for example, we start to regulate the breath, send more oxygen to the body and guide the mind and body into a more relaxed state. When we cultivate the ability to manage our internal state using our breath, regardless of what's going on outside of us, we then have a skill that has unlimited value.

The breath is also what connects us to the Divine every passing moment and sustains our life. Learning to quiet the mind and ride the wave of the breath flowing in and out can allow us to learn how to ride the ups and downs in life with more comfort. The breath is our life force energy and so by engaging in powerful pranayama techniques such as Kapalabhati Breath or the Breath of Joy, we can increase our life force energy and clear the mind. There are also specific methods of using pranayama that can arouse the Kundalini energy which lies dormant at the base of the spine. As the Kundalini energy moves up the spine, it clears through energetic blockages and activates the spiritual energy centers known as chakras. With the guidance of a trained teacher, this process of breathing and raising Kundalini energy begins to awaken your higher consciousness and provides a state of universal understanding and Divine connection. The Kundalini energy is creative energy and when activated and combined with meditation and intention can be used to co-create reality with the Divine. The key is to use the breath, or Prana, in an expansive way for this specific purpose.

At the same time, there are other Pranayama techniques that are designed to calm and quiet the mind by balancing the two hemispheres of the brain. Nadi Shodhan or Alternate Nostril Breath is a practice of inhaling through the right nostril and exhaling through the left, and then inhaling through the left and exhaling through the right nostril. Typically, this process would be repeated for five to ten minutes to start. This purification synchronizes the brain as it brings oxygen to both hemispheres and allows for one to move into an alpha brain wave state as well. The practice also brings balance to the body, clearing blocked energy channels and releasing stress and tension. Alternate Nostril Breath is also used to decrease one's anxiety which can ultimately allow one to feel more connected to the present moment and Divine support. This is just one of many pranayama or breath control techniques that yogis use to gain more control of the mind and body. And like anything, the more one practices pranayama techniques the more effective they become.

And finally, relaxation is another vital component of the practice of yoga. At the end of most yoga classes, you will be provided the opportunity to relax in what is called "savasana", which literally translates as "corpse pose". Although the name of the pose sounds a little morbid, it is a vital component to the practice and can be the most difficult of poses for some people. Being asked to simply lie on your back on a yoga mat and do nothing can initially be challenging for people whose minds typically are racing with thoughts or find themselves busy and on the go all the time. To the goal driven individual, it may seem at first that they're not accomplishing anything, but the state of relaxation experienced while in the pose is important for the brain. During the rest of the yoga practice, new neural pathways are being formed as the individual holds various asanas and deepens their awareness and connection to their physical body. The brain is also changing when the individual is practicing pranayama techniques that are new to them. Savasana is the pose, the time, and the opportunity for those new neural pathways to strengthen their connection and deepen the groove in the record.

Savasana is also the time for the brain to enter a more relaxed brain wave state such as Alpha or Theta, depending on the length of time provided and the ability of the individual to let go. This time allows the brain to not only integrate the yoga practice but sometimes also experiences from their day or even experiences from earlier in life. Sometimes unprocessed or unresolved emotions become stored in the physical body during childhood and adulthood and are held there at a physical and energetic level. The physical poses in yoga can begin to shift and move these stored emotions which can come to the surface to be processed when the mind is finally still and quiet in savasana. Again, yoga is the process of peeling through the layers of the onion and the layers of emotions and experiences we've had so that we can connect to the Divinity within us that lies beneath all of that. Savasana is one of the magical places where we can discover that as the mind and body relax into the present moment. Other more profound experiences can also occur in savasana, which are always unique to the individual.

Coming to know and understand the "oneness" of all things is possible when in a relaxed state in savasana. Even more profound is the experience of sensing that all things are intricately connected in this Divine web of the universe and that you are the other person and the other person is you. On three separate occasions, I have been blessed to have such an experience. The first time was in savasana at the end of a Qi Kung class, where the instructor came around to make some adjustments. I was lying on my back and he was standing near my head and leaned over to place his hands on my shoulders, encouraging them to soften and relax. As my energetic field merged with his energetic field there was a moment of oneness. The most significant experience though was that in that moment I felt that I was him and he was me and that we were not separate in any way. It almost felt that I was leaning over, helping and adjusting myself. Again, a few years later, in savasana at the end of a yoga class, the instructor came around to make a very similar adjustment. Kindly and gently, she slipped a blanket under my head and upper shoulders and invited me to surrender into the support. In that moment, my experience felt so significant and deep that it was unforgettable. I was her and she was me and we were in a total union. I only remember feeling as though I was looking down at myself and helping myself as if I were the instructor. I recall the thought that it was so nice of me to help myself. The only way that this could make sense is from the perspective that we are all one and intricately connected.

The next time the experience occurs it is even deeper still. At the end of another yoga class, the instructor comes around to gently adjust and massage my feet for a few moments. He is guiding the class to relax deeper into savasana at the time, verbally inviting each to scan their body for tension and release into their mat. As he does so, I enter into a deeply relaxed state where it feels like there is nothing but darkness, empty space and pure vibration. The vibration seemed to expand large enough to fill the entire room. It was similar to the experience of being within the interconnected web of the Divine Universe that I had a few months earlier when I was guided to that place by Spirit. This time, I not only recognize and experience that I am the yoga instructor and that the yoga instructor is me, but that I am everyone in the room and that everyone in the room is me. That we are not separate in any way, shape or form. We are all completely united as one. There were approximately 30 people in the room at the time but at the same time, there was only one. Not one "person" but one collective consciousness. Now, I had read many books and understood intellectually that we are "all one" but to have the actual experience of this feeling truly blew my mind wide open in a wonderful way. I can now say with complete certainty that this is true. This magical, beautiful and magnificent experience changed my world view permanently and forever.

This is not necessarily what happens for everyone during the practice of yoga. The overall practice is simply that…a practice which can only ever be unique to the individual. There are infinite transformational experiences that can happen for an individual during the practice of yoga, some of which can be very profound or allow one to feel more connected to the

Divine. The experience, awakening or moment of awareness could happen during asana, pranayama, meditation or savasana. The only requirement is to show up on your yoga mat, as often as you can, with an open mind, an open heart and a dedication to the Divine aspect within yourself. It is recommended that you avoid trying to make something profound happen or have any expectations of what you might experience. The key instead is just to be open to the many layers that will be peeled back and revealed to you as you continue to practice yoga and remind yourself to enjoy the journey because that's all there is anyway!

CHAPTER 10:

CONCLUSION – THE DANCE PERFORMANCE

So now it's time to perform and put all those dance steps into action every day in your life! You're officially on the Awareness Train now but please remember that this trip on the Awareness Train is infinite. That you are meant to enjoy the ride and you are meant to learn to dance with the Divine along the way. There will be bumps and curves along this train ride so please don't expect it to be consistently smooth. In fact, you may not realize it, but you wouldn't want things to be perfectly smooth all the time on the train ride or on the dance floor of life. Why not? Because if you never experience any bumps in the road or slips on the dance floor than you would never learn or grow or evolve. Just like the seed that must break through its shell and then push through the soil to eventually feel the warmth of the sun as it blossoms, you too need to experience challenges and a similar birthing process to allow your soul to expand into its fullest potential.

As you learn to dance or prepare for your dance performance you may trip and fall, or you may feel nervous before you go on stage. And when you are experiencing a challenging time or crisis in your life, it is important to remember to ask the question "how can I find the gift in this challenge?" because everything in your life is for your spiritual growth. It at least

241

has the potential to be part of your spiritual growth. If you perceive the challenge or crisis from the viewpoint of a victim, then there is no growth or lesson learned. If you perceive the challenge as an opportunity to grow and look for the gift, then it will become a spiritual blessing. Living in a state of benevolence means that you have come to realize that there are good times in life and there are challenging times but that at the deepest level it is all good because life is simply a journey back home to connect with the Source or the Divine. Make a conscious choice to see everything in your life as part of your spiritual awakening and your life will be a blessing. It is only when we embrace the shadow and the darkness that the light can emerge. We need the contrast of darkness in order be the light. And when the crisis or the challenge arises in your life and you feel as though you're in a dark place, remember that you can always ask the Divine to help you find your way back to the light. You can allow yourself to be carried in the arms of the Divine and be shown the way.

Whenever you feel lost or frustrated or hopeless, I can promise you that the Divine is still within you and all around you, waiting for you to connect, so that it may support you. I will always remember my trip to a meditation retreat in Toronto of 2018. I decided to head out to go Salsa dancing after a long day of sitting at the workshop and sitting during meditation. I was thinking all day about going to my favorite restaurant "Fresh" at some point during the week-long retreat. After Salsa dancing, I was starving so I checked Google to find out where the nearest Fresh Restaurant was, but the search indicated that all the locations closed at 10 pm and it was now

10:03 pm. I was sad and disappointed as I had been looking forward all day to eating there. Dismayed, I headed back to my hotel in hopes of finding a place to grab a quick sub or something. I parked my car underground at the hotel, went out and walked up to street level and the Divine whispered, "Go right, Carol." So, I trusted the Divine and went right. I walked past the Keg and an Irish Pub thinking that was not what I wanted at this time of night. The Divine whispered again, "Go left at the corner Carol." Of course, I obliged. Tim Hortons and Subway were both closed. It was only a moment of frustration before the Divine nudged once more, "Go left at the top of this hill, Carol. You're almost there." I responded of course by going left at the top of the hill and then just past a Moroccan restaurant was a glass door that was wide open to another place. I felt the Divine smile down on me, so I stopped and looked at the glass door. The name and logo on the door made my heart sing! It was Fresh!! A new Fresh location that just happened to be open till 11 pm! Imagine that! I walked in and sat down at a table with my heart beaming and ordered my favorite meal as it was now 10:30 pm. I spoke with the waitress about how long the location had been open. She explained that it had only been a month and probably not even coming up on a google search yet. I enjoyed every moment of my meal and felt grateful for the Divine for being patient with me during the process. I even brought my friends from the workshop back the next night for dinner to make sure the place was there, and it wasn't just happening all in my mind! I was initially discouraged when I thought there was no Fresh location open, but I was lovingly reminded that when we let go and trust Divine Guidance, our concerns can be handled by the Divine in ways that are unbeknownst to us.

Hopefully, you have realized along the way that the Divine is all around you, all the time, waiting to support you and guide you on your journey. The Divine essence has always been with you and always will be with you. It is all around you and it is within you and within all other beings and all other living things. This Divine essence is also known as "consciousness" is only wanting and waiting patiently to become aware of itself. In actuality, you are both the individual expression of this Divine consciousness as well as the universal expression of this consciousness…at the same time. Consciousness uses the physical body as a vehicle so that it may be able to see itself. When you are looking at another person it is like looking in a mirror. And when you and another person are fully present in the moment and making eye contact with each other, the Divine essence that lies within both people will recognize itself. And that feeling feels like coming home. You will know it when it happens because there is no other feeling like it in the world. The Divine essence within you comes to experience the world and to simply be, not to "do" and be busy all the time. The process of connecting with this Divine essence obviously requires being fully present in the moment and working through the layers, like peeling an onion.

Peeling through these layers of beliefs and concepts and ego identity requires dedication to constantly be doing the work. Those who brave the challenge and choose to get on this Awareness Train need to be recognized for their strength and courage. When you arrived on this planet, as an infant, you were without any identity or beliefs and were more connected to the Divine essence. That's why when you look deep into the eyes of an infant you can see purity and clarity. Their eyes are clear and present as they take in their environment and the world around them. Layer by layer, one experience after another, beliefs get developed, an identity is created and a world of repetitive thoughts becomes manifested into reality. The only way back home and back to dancing with the Divine is to get on the Awareness Train and peel back the very same layers that were created one at a time. Question your beliefs that are not serving you, take the time to challenge and change those beliefs so that you may come to realize that you are the Divine co-creator of your own life.

This peeling back of the layers and the changing of beliefs is the process of letting go of who you think you are and blossoming into who you desire to become and getting closer to the Divine along the way. Although the process can be difficult at times, there is never any doubt that it is worth the effort. And during the darkest and most challenging times you can rest assured that if you ask for help, the Divine will carry you through it. There is nothing to fear during the darkest times as the light is just around the corner at that point.

"Just when the caterpillar thought the world was over…it became a butterfly." ~ Anonymous ~

Our fear of change can be ignited when we are in transition from the caterpillar to the butterfly. However, asking to connect with the Divine during this time and allowing yourself to trust the process is what can lead to synchronistic events, magic, and miracles in your life. And then the process of spreading your wings to become the butterfly is full of more elegance and beauty. Trusting the Divine and being open to receiving the support, as it comes in ways that you least expect is the most important part. Relax into the arms of the Divine, open your heart and give yourself permission to grow into who you were meant to become in this lifetime.

Applying the steps is the other important part of the process of change. The work is in recognizing and accepting that you cannot control everything in the world outside of yourself and that it can be exhausting if you attempt to do so. Once you come to realize that in order to change your world you only need to take control over your own thoughts, beliefs, and emotions, then you have taken back 100% of your power. As you practice and learn to manage your mind and your state of being, using Emotional Freedom Technique, Yoga and Meditation, then and only then will your whole world change in ways that you can't possibly imagine. Couple that with allowing yourself to believe in something greater, such as the Divine, opening and welcoming synchronistic events into your life and learning to be led on the dance floor of life and you've got one magical way of living! Remember that it is an ever-unfolding practice, so enjoy the ride. Hence, your final dance steps include…

Step 1: Become aware of your thought patterns and belief systems that are not serving you in your life and empower yourself to change your reality from the inside out.

Step 2: Use Emotional Freedom Technique, Yoga and Meditation to transform and transcend those limiting thoughts and beliefs.

Step 3: Look for the miracles, magic and synchronistic events in your life to strengthen your belief in the power and support of the Divine during this process.

Step 4: Love, laugh and let go so that the Divine may lead you on the dance floor of life!

May you enjoy dancing with the Divine every step of the way! May you move in rhythm together and flow effortlessly with grace and ease. Many blessings on your journey.

P.S. This book was written while listening to very specific music, for a very specific reason.

In the background, on repeat, for hours on end, played "Ode to Joy" from Beethoven's 9th Symphony, guiding me with every word that poured from my fingertips onto the page. I would encourage you to look up the English version of the lyrics to "Ode to Joy" as they provide a beautiful message. My favorite line is "Can you sense the Creator, world?" Because this "Creator" is always within you and all around you.

The words in this book were also born while listening over and over to Hallelujah by K.D. Lang and Amazing Grace as sung by LeAnn Rimes, both songs, of course, radiating the love and light of the Divine.

The other specific music that was listened to at the time of writing is an album called "Flow of Naam" produced by Gurunaam Joseph Michael Levry. This album can be found on www.rootlight.com and is able to help one develop higher powers. Vibrating this sacred sound current has the potential to turn you into a center of radiance and magnetic energy. It leads to the development of a benevolent, magnetic personality and radiant spirit. Each mantra on the album is quite powerful and magical in its own way.

The reason that this specific music was listened to while writing is simple…when one is listening to the music of the Divine, one begins to vibrate AS the Divine. As one begins to vibrate AS the Divine, the words that come through, during the process of writing can only be those words that resonate with the teachings and wisdom of the Divine. It is my deepest desire that you can feel the love of the Divine coming through on this page as you read it. May you be blessed with love, magic, miracles and a life more beautiful than you can possibly imagine.

Manufactured by Amazon.ca
Bolton, ON

23697358R00146